THE COST OF
WINNING

THE COST OF WINNING

COMING IN **FIRST** ACROSS THE **WRONG** FINISH LINE

DEAN HUGHES

DESERET
BOOK
SALT LAKE CITY, UTAH

For Cory Maxwell,
editor and friend

Library of Congress Cataloging-in-Publication Data

Hughes, Dean, 1943–
    The cost of winning : coming in first across the wrong finish line / Dean Hughes.
        p.   cm.
    Includes bibliographical references and index.
    ISBN 978-1-59038-910-2 (paperbound)
    1. Christian life—Mormon authors.   I. Title.
    BX8656.H84 2008
    248.4'89332—dc22   2008005289

Printed in the United States of America
Sheridan Books Inc., Ann Arbor, MI

10   9   8   7   6   5   4   3   2   1

Contents

CHAPTER 1

The Confusing World We Live In

I DON'T ALWAYS THINK STRAIGHT. I suspect that most of us don't. And yet, the way we think about life makes a huge difference in how things turn out for us. When we get confused about what we're trying to do—about life's purpose—we get ourselves into a terrible muddle.

Every now and then I experience something that jars me, that opens my eyes to just how fouled up our values can get. I had that kind of experience a few years ago at a youth-league baseball game. One afternoon I thought I'd walk over to our neighborhood park and watch an inning or two—just to remind myself of the atmosphere. I was writing a series of children's books about baseball, and I wanted to be as authentic as possible. But as I approached the diamond, I witnessed something I could hardly believe. Four men, probably in their late thirties, were standing near first base. They were leaning over a low fence toward the infield as far as they could, and they were bellowing in fanatic voices: "You can't throw a strike, kid! You *know* you can't. You're gonna walk this guy!"

On the mound was a chunky boy, maybe eleven, who was staring at his catcher. I noticed also that the bases were loaded. A walk would force in a run.

The players on the bench were shouting, too, and so were some of the spectators, but the four adults were drowning out all the other voices. "You *can't* throw a strike! You *know* you're gonna walk him!"

The boy did throw a bad pitch and the men yelped with joy. Then they started the chant again. They kept it up until the pitcher, as predicted, threw a fourth ball, which forced in the run.

All the boys on the batter's team cheered, and the four men went wild, clapping and shouting, and then they started again. "You'll walk this next guy, too. You *know* you can't throw strikes!"

But the pitcher, a big boy for his age, was standing with his arms folded, and I could see that he was losing his fight with his emotions. His chest began to heave as he broke down. His coach walked out to the mound, put his arm around the boy's shoulders, talked to him for a few seconds, and then sent him to the bench—to the cheers of the four men, who were apparently proud of themselves. Another boy trotted in from the outfield to take over the pitching, but now the same guys were on another rant. "Hey, kid, what makes you think *you* can pitch? You can't throw strikes, either." I thought the umpire might go over and tell them to stop, but he didn't. No parents objected either. So I left.

I decided I didn't want my children's books to be *that* authentic. It seemed just as well that I keep my memories—however idealized they may be—of how baseball was when I was a boy.

But I've always regretted that I didn't go over and ask those four men what they thought they were doing. Maybe they would have told me that they were preparing that young pitcher for the pressures he would have to face in life. Or maybe they would have said, "Hey, it's all part of the game."

But chances are, they hadn't really thought it through that far. They were fathers of players, I'm sure, and they wanted their boys to win. They saw a way to make it happen. After all, "Winning isn't everything; it's the only thing." Didn't Vince Lombardi teach us that?

And haven't we bought into that mentality?

This may have been an extreme example, but I don't see an awful lot of what we used to call "good sportsmanship" at the athletic events I attend these days. Our society is becoming increasingly profane and increasingly committed to winning at any cost. Most people wouldn't be as severe as these fathers were, but hasn't taunting become basic to sports fans?

If a basketball player takes a shot and misses the hoop entirely, what are we supposed to yell? Every fan knows the answer: "Air ball! Air ball!" Shouted in a spirit of derision and glee, it's the standard chant, and you'll hear it at every game, including those played at Brigham Young University.

That's not so bad, is it? It's just fun.

My guess is, it's a lot more fun if you're *not* the player who took the shot.

It's also great fun when your team clearly has the victory in hand to sing, "Na, na, na, na. Na, na, na, na. Hey, hey, hey, good-bye."

But have you noticed? It's rather galling when it's your team getting hammered and all those fans on the other side are taunting *you*.

Does this suggest that we are becoming ever more crass as a people? Are we developing attitudes and behaviors we hardly recognize, but ones that lead to disrespect and unkindness? Am I asking too much, or couldn't we back off a little in all the put-downs and insults we've become so fond of hurling at each other? It just seems to me that sports could be played in an atmosphere of good-natured friendship.

This is not a book about sports, but in many ways our behavior at sporting events illustrates a problem that I see getting worse all the time in our society. We take many of our metaphors for life from athletics, and we often describe life as though it's a game— something you win or lose. You know the term for that: "The game of life."

But here's the part that interests me most. The baseball game I described was played in Provo, Utah. It took place in a part of town where probably ninety percent of the people are members of The Church of Jesus Christ of Latter-day Saints. So how could four adults, possibly all priesthood holders, think it was a good idea to harass a child until he cracked? And then, after watching him break into tears, go to work on the next child? If we were to follow the logic all the way to its roots, I think it comes back to that Lombardi concept that winning is not just good, but "everything."

Life, after all, is a contest.

But is it?

Who said so?

Did Christ ever teach anything like that?

I was teaching an adult Sunday School class some years back, and I asked the students to describe a "good Mormon." I got answers that had to do with compliance: church attendance, adherence to the laws of tithing and the Word of Wisdom, willingness to serve in Church callings, and so forth. But then I asked, "What comes to mind when I say, 'Good Christian'?"

I got different answers.

People talked about service, kindness, love, and looking after one's neighbor. It's worried me ever since to think that the answers differed as much as they did. It seems to me that the question for us should always be, "Am I a follower of Christ? And if I am, how should I live?"

Even at a baseball game.

Here's the truth, as I understand it. I think it's what Christ taught. Life is *not* a contest. It's not a free-for-all, with each person pitted against everyone else. I'm convinced that much of what's wrong in our world comes from thinking that it is.

I suspect that most people, when asked directly, would actually agree with me. They would tell me that we can all live together in happiness. We can support one another, think the best of each other, and act for the good of the whole community. But when theory moves to practice, we have a tendency to play by the rules of our culture rather than by the spirit of Christ's teachings.

I've been thinking a lot about life lately, at least partly because I've passed into that dreadful world of Over Sixty, and I think that's changed my perspective. What I wish is that I'd sorted certain things out sooner. It won't be long now—a blink of an eye, from an eternal perspective—before I stand before the Lord and answer for my life. If I had done some better thinking, sooner, I suspect I'd now be more the person I'd like to be. True, mere thinking won't get us where we want to go, but if we start with the all the wrong assumptions, we're in danger of expending our energies pursuing the wrong objectives.

I don't mean to pretend that I suddenly have great wisdom simply because I'm a senior citizen. If I were *really* wise, I'd probably write a long treatise. Maybe I'll try that when I'm eighty or ninety. For now, this is just a little book—to match the scope of my wisdom.

My baseball story implies something more. That boy—the young pitcher—represents all of us in certain ways. We're doing our best, and the world is shouting at us, telling us what we're worth, what we can do and *can't* do. I think a lot of us spend our lives feeling that we *can't* throw strikes. We try so hard, and sometimes it seems that the more effort we put out, the worse we do. I have some thoughts about that—how we can deal with some of that noise coming out of the grandstands—but before I get to that, I want to see if I can define some of the challenges I think we're facing.

It seems to me that one of the great challenges is to understand mortality while we're still in the middle of it. We face a lot of worldly influences that we don't always recognize. In fact, I fear that we try to make certain ideas and values fit with the gospel of Jesus Christ when they simply don't.

My wife, Kathy, and I recently took our three-year-old grandson Sam shopping. He made a purchase with his own money, and the clerk gave him back some change. He liked that. He got the stuff he wanted, plus the clerk returned to him *more* money. He looked up at us with his gapped-tooth smile and said, "I *wike* money!"

Of course he does. All those toys he finds in the stores, and the ones advertised on television—he can have every one of them. All he needs is money.

Do we ever grow up?

The toys get bigger. Instead of Transformers and superheroes, we want snowmobiles and boats, fancy cars and fancy houses. But we never stop wanting "stuff."

We go to the mall and we see something—some wonderful widget—and we tell ourselves we have to have it. It's not just any widget; it's made of *quality* plastic. And it's fancier than all the widgets in the neighborhood. So we save up and we get that widget and it pleases us immensely. But stores have lots of widgets, and while we're buying ours, we notice that there's a "high end" widget that would *really* be fantastic to own: a big screen, hi-speed, digitized, *glorious* widget. After all, the family down the street has now raised the bar: they just got the new, improved *titanium* widget. We have to fight back! So we make that next purchase, bring it home in triumph, and we show off our prize to all the neighbors.

What joy!

But there are always more widgets. And the contest continues to escalate. Thank goodness, we've discovered that there's a shorter route to happiness—one that doesn't require us to wait. We can use plastic to buy our plastic widgets; it works at all the stores. Forget the debt; I've got my stuff!

The irony is, we keep telling ourselves, "Money can't buy happiness. What really matters to me is family, faith, and friends." And we believe it. We *know* it's true. But, oh, those widgets. They have siren voices, and they call to us when we drive past the mall. We know they're in there—on sale this week—and if we don't get them, someone else will.

It's our way of life, isn't it? We work hard so we'll have enough money. We spend more than we make, which means we have to work even harder just to keep up with the bills we've created. And then we get old, and we look around our houses and we say, "What am I going to do with all these widgets?" So we offer them to our children, who say, "No thanks. They're making better widgets now—made out of *platinum*—and I have a card (a *platinum* card) that will buy me anything I want. Throw away your widgets, Mom and Pop. We wouldn't have those old things in our house."

Styles change. And it's very bad to own things that are out of style. Who doesn't know that? Throw out last year's clothes. Get new ones that look strangely like the stuff that was in style twenty years ago.

(By the way, have you ever asked yourself who decides what's "cool," what's "the latest," what's "in style"? Don't get me wrong. I'm old, but, hey, I'm stylish. I was just wondering, that's all.)

The name for our behavior—all this desire for widgets and stylish things—is, of course, *materialism.* It's based on the idea that if you want something, you ought to go after it and get it, because getting things makes us happy. Of course, it never works—not for very long—but we don't seem to learn that until we've used up our lives chasing after "stuff."

Buddhists see this whole thing the other way around. As they explain it, the problem is in the wanting—the perpetual desire to have things. *Wanting* leads to unhappiness, and *acquiring* never stops the pain. So the answer is to overcome the wanting. That attitude is absolutely foreign to most people in the Western world, who believe the road to happiness is paved with lovely widgets. We confuse *want* with *need,* and we think we'll be happier when the want is satisfied.

But listen to what Christ taught: "Lay not up for yourselves treasures upon earth, where moth and rust doth corrupt, and where thieves break through and steal: But lay up for yourselves treasures in heaven, where neither moth nor rust doth corrupt, and where thieves do not break through nor steal: *For where your treasure is, there will your heart be also*" (Matthew 6:19–21; emphasis added).

And, of course, we know He's right.

Materialism doesn't come from Christ.

Notice that our motivation is all too often not just to have nice things, but to use those things to compete: to gain status, to demonstrate success, to establish supremacy.

One of the odd things about life is that when we chase after possessions, we know we're in a false pursuit, but we find ways to justify ourselves. As Latter-day Saints, we place emphasis on the family, so maybe it's natural to feel that a nice home is necessary, and maybe large families require larger homes. But our tendency to rate our own success and the success of others by the size (and sometimes the extravagance) of our homes has, ironically, often led us into excessive debt that becomes destabilizing to the very families we seek to serve.

I think the important thing to remember is that the problem with materialism is not that we try to make a good living and then buy the things we need; it's the false hope that we can extract more from worldly "treasures" than material goods can possibly provide. It's the self-indulgent child in us that looks in the store window and says, "I just need one of those, and then I won't ask for anything else." We all know how long that promise lasts.

I think most of us hope to achieve a certain "status" in the world. It seems rather natural to hope to further our talents, do something significant with our lives. But many of us are *driven* to achieve. We feel a need to win, to excel, to be noticed. We thrive on our triumphs, thrill to seeing our names in the newspaper, or feel good about ourselves when we get a promotion or a raise. But the satisfaction doesn't last. We soon feel the need to notch another victory. The danger in this attitude is that it leads to a self-centered life. It's not easy for us to love our neighbors when we harbor a hidden desire to be "above" them in the social pecking order. We seem to fear that importance is a limited commodity, that there's only so much of it to go around. It's as though people who rise in the world push us down in some imaginary ranking system.

The quest for importance, the way it's pursued in our world, never seems to have an end. And part of the reason is that importance has to come from the mind and perception of someone else. When we set out to become important, we grant others the right to assess our value, and then we worry whether enough people grant us the status we long for. But fame often means that one in a hundred might actually know our names, and people who hunger for importance remain heartsick that the other ninety-nine don't recognize them as they walk by.

The race to feel important is deeply competitive and inherently prideful. It also backfires on us. Someone is always "above" us, so no matter our perceived status, we end up feeling painfully ordinary. It's as though our emotional needs, without conscious awareness, enter us in a contest—and we're losing.

President Ezra Taft Benson gave a landmark talk on the evils of pride, in which he quoted C. S. Lewis, who observed: "Pride gets no pleasure out of having something, only out of having more of it than the next man. We say that people are proud of being rich, or clever, or good-looking, but they are not. They are proud of being richer, or cleverer, or better-looking than others. If everyone else became equally rich, or clever, or good-looking there would be nothing to be proud about. It is the comparison that makes you proud: the pleasure of being above the rest. Once the element of competition has gone, pride has gone" (*Mere Christianity* [New York: Macmillan, 1952], 109; "Beware of Pride," *Ensign*, May 1989, 4).

And that's the problem, isn't it? We think we have to outdo others, but there's always someone richer or more famous or more important. The comparison process ultimately leads to a sense of our own relative worthlessness. Victories make us feel important, but no one wins all the time, and when we measure our worth by the world's standards for wins and losses, any loss seems to be magnified. The result can only be a sense of defeat.

Don't misunderstand what I'm saying. The gospel teaches us to improve ourselves, to make eternal progress. We believe in devoting ourselves to self-improvement, growing, developing our talents, and becoming more like God. It's comparing ourselves to other people that creates the problem, not the rate of our own personal progress.

And here's an irony: if we become *self*-absorbed in our drive to improve ourselves, we go backwards, not forwards. One of the challenges of living the Christ-like life is that we can only inherit the kingdom of God by forgetting ourselves. We're not going to succeed by an ego-based drive to knock down the door of heaven—and to get there ahead of everyone else.

Being "driven" for success is something we hear praised. Most of us envy high achievers so much that it's hard not to think that almost any sacrifice would be worth the victories we imagine. But to God, is anyone more important than anyone else? And if we commit ourselves to some worldly pursuit that consumes all our energy and attention, don't we stand in danger of losing focus on what *really* matters?

We know our real purpose in life: to keep our covenants with God, to *become* the person the Lord would want us to be. But in a subtle way, we can enter into a competition that should never exist. Have you ever wondered why Sister So-'n-So got called to serve as Relief Society president when you've never had the chance? Or why you've been stuck in the clerk's office all your life when you could have been a good bishop? There are many versions of this kind of thinking: We listen to the brother in testimony meeting talk about all his children having served missions and having been married in the temple and we wonder why that's not true for us; we wonder why a certain couple has never been all that committed to church service and tithing and, still, they prosper economically; we see a certain sister who's kind and good and beautiful and well-dressed and *everything else,* and we wonder why she got *all* the gifts and we received far fewer; we hear a brother bear powerful, unwavering testimony, and we wonder why doubt plagues our own thoughts.

You see what I'm talking about: a temptation, even in the Church, to compete with one another. Maybe it slips into our minds that the Lord must love someone else more than He loves us, or at least we wonder why life can't be fair.

Given the complexity of comparing one life to another, how can we ever see things from God's perspective? It seems crucial that we accept our lives, our gifts, our opportunities, our challenges, and not compare. A ward can only be strong when members think well of one another, take joy in one another's prosperity, and freely forgive those who have offended them. The problem is, we're human, and no ward ever attains a perfect level of love. All the same, when we're thinking about life correctly, we aren't justifying our jealousy and unkindness. When we remember that a ward, of all places, should never be a site of competition, we have a better chance of avoiding those feelings.

I hope I'm not the only one who feels that something is wrong. Human values have almost always been out of sync with the Lord's wishes for us, but it seems to me that the divide has never been greater. We're constantly enticed to place too much focus on acquiring material things—and to prove our status by a drive to grab more than other "contestants." We seek importance, and we trust in the false definitions of worth that the world has devised for us. We spend our lives seeking achievement, again defined by the world, and that certainly isn't all bad, but we devote so much of our emphasis on those worldly achievements that we give too little attention to *becoming* the persons we actually want to be. And all this competitiveness leads us away from Christ instead of toward Him.

What Christ offers is peace. But the irony is, escaping the contest I've been describing may be the only way we can ever feel that peace.

I'm afraid we try to trick ourselves into believing that we can lay up treasures on earth and in heaven at the same time—without losing our hearts. But Christ has warned us about that, and we need to listen.

I said in the beginning that I don't always think straight. But I'm trying. I think we all need to try. I feel certain that we need to get some false ways of looking at life *out* of our heads so that we can let the teachings of Jesus Christ *in*.

This book is about Christ and what He taught us. It's about sorting out what the world is screaming at us and recognizing the false pursuits we tend to engage in. It's about finding peace.

I don't think many of us are entirely on the *wrong* path. We haven't given over our hearts to evil. But our grasp on the iron rod is loose at times, and we're paying far too much attention to all those folks in that big building on the other side of the river. We're making life far more complicated than it needs to be. The simple path—the straight and the strait one—just feels better. We recognize it with every footfall, and the vibrations run through us directly to the spirit within us. It's the contest that we don't need. Life is so much better when we stay out of it.

And it *is* a choice.

I'm not promoting one more self-improvement project, one more reason to feel guilty. I'm actually saying that we can let go of some of the pressure in our lives. We can *stop* pushing ourselves so hard—stop feeling defeated, left behind. We can simplify the way we live. We can feel more in tune with God, more comfortable with who we are, happier than we've ever been.

We really can find peace. His peace.

Chapter 2

Our Divided Selves

WE TELL OUR KIDS, "YOU'VE gotta have a dream." It's such standard advice that we never think to question it. The formula is, a young person should dream big and then go after that dream. But what is it they'll get if they dream big and devote all their efforts to getting what they want?

That's not quite so clear.

I suppose "success" would be the answer. But reaching success depends a great deal on what a person thinks life is all about. That's what we talked about in the first chapter. Now let's look at where this confusion about our priorities leads us and determine what we can do about it.

When I was serving as a bishop, I used to ask the young men and women in my ward how they pictured themselves in ten years—what they would be doing with their lives. They knew the right answers: They wanted to fill missions, get married in the temple, start a family. But if I asked what they "dreamed" of doing in their lives, many of them became animated, and then they talked about the goals that really excited them.

Some were enthusiastic about certain careers; some wanted to develop their talents as musicians, dancers, or athletes; many wanted to "make a mark" in the world in some way. If I questioned them long enough, I found that the idea of gaining fame was actually enticing, although they hesitated to admit it. They usually spoke idealistically about money. "That's not the most important thing to me," they would say. And yet, they liked to envision themselves living in beautiful homes, and some would admit to the desire for fancy cars. So they didn't call it "having money," but they clearly wanted to have the things that money could buy.

And in one way or another, most of the young people had the same feeling I'd had at their age. They wanted to be "somebody" in this world. They wanted to succeed, and their definitions of success usually followed standard American definitions.

Is that bad? I don't think so. But there are some hidden dangers—some subtle implications about the placement of their hearts.

Fame. Wealth. Power. They all sound ugly and prideful when we admit that we find them attractive. And so we learn to speak of "being successful," of "reaching goals," or of "having a positive influence in the world." Then we quickly add that if we made some money, we would like to use it to help others. That certainly can happen, but it's almost funny how ingenious we are at denying that we want the very things that the world holds up as the rewards for success.

Not once, during all the time I was bishop, did I ever have a teenager tell me: "In ten years I'd like to be really meek and humble. That's what I'm working on now. My kindness, my charity, my humility."

Why are you laughing?

If at the end of our lives, our humility and goodness are going to be the measure of our success in the Lord's eyes, why does it seem almost comical to imagine young people striving after those very traits? I don't think most of us have thought this through very carefully, but aren't we divided between what we *say* is important to us and what we *demonstrate* is important by our actions?

That's what I've been thinking about.

I'm not a philosopher, an economist, or a theologian. My analysis may not be very sophisticated. But I started to notice something in myself and others a long time ago, and it has become increasingly clear to me as years have gone by. In many countries of the world—but especially in the United States—we adhere to two strong and yet, in many ways, opposite value systems. We love them both, and we often find ways to connect them, but we also sense at times that they're an awkward fit.

The majority of Americans profess a belief in Jesus Christ, and almost all Americans believe in free enterprise. We often speak of these two philosophical systems as though they're a hand-in-glove match. And in some ways maybe they are. But why is it we feel a little nervous about the interplay of the two every year at Christmastime?

Think about it. Have you ever heard anyone say that the Fourth of July "is just too commercialized"?

On Independence Day, we praise freedom and liberty, and we're referring to all our freedoms, but one of them is the free-market system or capitalism, which is unquestionably better, in our minds, than socialistic economic systems.

So why is it that as Christmas approaches, we like to blame the stores for corrupting our holy celebration? Those terrible stores "commercialize" Christmas.

I've now gone through about sixty Christmas seasons that I can remember, and I started noticing almost from the beginning that people always say, "The stores are putting up their Christmas decorations earlier than ever this year." If the decorations really had come out earlier each one of those sixty years, by now the Christmas season would begin in July. I just don't think the starting date has changed as drastically as we think it has.

But the question is, why does that perception bother us so much?

Suppose you owned a company that made a nicely built, time-saving, everyone-needs-one product. And suppose you noticed that people liked to buy these devices to give as Christmas presents. Considering that, wouldn't you hope to sell as many as possible during this peak season so that you could feed your family the rest of the year?

Is that commercialism?

Of course it is.

But that's a good thing, isn't it? It's free enterprise. It's the capitalist system we Americans embrace so lovingly. President Benson, who worried about the pride of comparing and competing with others, championed the virtue of competitiveness in our economic system:

> A free market survives with competition. Were it not for more competition among goods or services, there could be no standard by which a buyer could discern shoddy merchandise or inept service from excellence. Were it not for competition, the seller could price his goods and services according to his own fancy. It is competition that determines what is good, better, and best. It is competition that determines the price for products or services. If goods are overpriced in comparison with other comparable goods,

the buyer will refuse to buy, thus forcing the seller to drop his price. [*This Nation Shall Endure* (Salt Lake City: Deseret Book Company, 1979), 108]

We agree with that, don't we, even if the system doesn't always work as perfectly as we might like? Sometimes advertising hypes things we don't really need. Powerful corporations can control the marketplace in unfair ways. Poorly built products sometimes find their way to buyers under the cover of misleading claims. Still, we feel confident that a free-market approach is much better than any system that is controlled primarily by government.

So why is it, during the holidays, we suddenly feel uneasy about businesses trying so hard to get their share of the money that's going to be spent on Christmas presents? What I suspect is that under the surface we all know that *we*, not the system, have made Christmas too materialistic. We know we spend too much money and that we've turned something sacred into, "What do you want for Christmas?"

What we believe is that Christmas ought to be simple, family-oriented, and peaceful. Instead it's hectic and worldly. But we keep doing it the same way each year. Many of us spend way too much money on gifts, go into debt, and realize every January—when the credit card bills come in—that we've gotten carried away.

But there's more to it than that. We say we like to give more than receive, and maybe we're somewhat disingenuous about that, but I do think we enjoy the giving. And in a materialistic society, maybe it's only natural that we would think that when it comes to giving, more is better—that we prove our love with the price of the present.

But we also give to the poor at that time of year— more than any other time. That's good, isn't it? The Christmas music, the stories, the "spirit of Christmas" does cause us to donate to Sub for Santa and other such charitable programs. We don't want any child to go without "a Christmas," as we call it. That's certainly a good impulse. Maybe we do try to manifest love with material gifts, but at least we include people in need.

But let's think about that, too. I once heard a United Way executive say that during the holidays Americans love to give a turkey to a poor family— *whether the family has an oven or not.* Sometimes, he said, it would be so much better to give that family a case of peanut butter—say, in August, when kids go back to school. But in August many of us don't think much about the poor. In August, we tend to get awfully worried about "the dole." A kind of every-man-for-himself mentality prevails. But Christmas is different. Everyone should have a Christmas—and that means *everyone* should get presents.

Is that materialism in the name of religion?

I think it is, but it's certainly not all bad. Some of our most noble emotions are inspired by the season, and maybe, instead of complaining so much about the commercialism, we should accept the two parts of ourselves represented by the frenzy we create.

We do need to operate in the economic world we live in. President Gordon B. Hinckley has often advised young people to prepare to compete in a tough environment:

> You face great challenges that lie ahead. You are moving into a world of fierce competition. You must get all of the education you can. The Lord has instructed us concerning the importance of education. It will qualify you for greater opportunities. It will equip you to do something worthwhile in the great world of opportunity that lies ahead. If you can go to college and that is your wish, then do it. If you have no desire to attend college, then go to a vocational or business school to sharpen your skills and increase your capacity. [Gordon B. Hinckley, "Converts and Young Men," *Ensign*, May 1997, 47]

At the same time, think of all the advice President Hinckley has given us about avoiding worldliness. It's a difficult line to walk, isn't it? We must operate in the competitive business world in order to make a living, but there are dangers in taking on the values that some in that world esteem. I said at the beginning that most of us struggle to think straight, and I'm convinced that one of the great divides in our lives is created by our attempt to mesh the competitive spirit of free enterprise with the cooperative spirit of Christianity.

America is the nation where we tell rags-to-riches stories as proof of the greatness of our system, and then we read the scriptures and notice that Jesus was not very impressed by riches—and possessed none Himself. This is also the nation where we're impressed by the "self-made man," which almost always means that he got rich. But in the next breath we'll accuse someone of "only doing it for the money," as though that's something shameful. How can we have it both ways?

I would say first that there is a difference between the competitiveness of the marketplace (which President Benson admired) and the individual competitiveness that takes joy only in ascending above others (which President Benson saw as prideful). Advertisers may try to convince us that we need certain products, but individuals decide whether they will spend more than they have, go to excess in their purchases, or use their possessions to show off. True, the system itself may imply that the purpose of life is mere "getting and spending," as William Wordsworth called it, but it's still a personal choice whether to value material goods above things of the spirit. In Wordsworth's words, "We have given our hearts away" ("The World Is Too Much with Us").

But can we resist? Can we successfully function in a society that places so much emphasis on acquisition and still live as Christ taught us to live? I think we can, but only if we sort out our confusion, get our thoughts clear, and in doing so, make our hearts right.

I have known people who started out on the right path, but success and money eventually became all important to them. At some point their values changed. They pushed for more and more wealth and power, and they became increasingly self-absorbed. They never had enough, no matter how much they accumulated, and they often indulged themselves in lifestyles that became self-destructive. They ended up selling their souls for a mess of pottage (see Genesis 25:29–34).

President Spencer W. Kimball warned us about the hazards of wealth:

> The Lord has blessed us as a people with a prosperity unequaled in times past. The resources that have been placed in our power are good, and necessary to our work here on the earth. But I am afraid that many of us have been surfeited with flocks and herds and acres and barns and wealth and have begun to worship them as false gods,

and they have power over us. . . . Forgotten is the fact that our assignment is to use these many resources in our families and quorums to build up the kingdom of God—to further the missionary effort and the genealogical and temple work; to raise our children up as fruitful servants unto the Lord; to bless others in every way, that they may also be fruitful. Instead, we expend these blessings on our own desires, and as Moroni said, "Ye adorn yourselves with that which hath no life, and yet suffer the hungry, and the needy, and the naked, and the sick and the afflicted to pass by you, and notice them not" (Morm. 8:39). [*Teachings of the Presidents of the Church: Spencer W. Kimball* (Salt Lake City: The Church of Jesus Christ of Latter-day Saints, 2006), 149]

Jacob, in the Book of Mormon, admonished his people about another danger of possessing wealth: "And the hand of providence hath smiled upon you most pleasingly, that you have obtained many riches; and because some of you have obtained more abundantly than that of your brethren ye are lifted up in the pride of your hearts, and wear stiff necks and high heads because of the costliness of your apparel, and persecute your brethren because ye suppose that ye are better than they" (Jacob 2:13).

In a competitive system, we all know there will be winners and losers. So how should we think about our brothers and sisters who don't have as much as we do—or, just as important, those who have much more? I once heard a Latter-day Saint say that his ward was divided between two neighborhoods—one in which most of the people were well off and the other one in which the economic level was considerably lower. His conclusion was that this mix didn't work—that the two different "sorts of people" didn't blend well.

He wasn't embarrassed or ashamed to tell me that.

I tried not to sound sarcastic as I suggested that a common love of the gospel just might be more important than the economic differences. But his opinion illustrates the problem that occurs when we stick two systems of thought together and then don't work at sorting out which one ought to prevail in a given situation. It's so important that we avoid carrying our competitive economic system over into our relations with our brothers and sisters.

I've seen it work the other way, too. I grew up in a family that didn't have much, and I heard people in my neighborhood—and I'll admit, in my own home—say harsh things about "rich people," who, we were certain, thought they were better than we were. It's a funny sort of irony that most people would like to become rich, and yet they resent those who have managed to accomplish it.

I love the atmosphere of the temple, where we all wear white, and no one seems more prominent, more important, or higher in "station" than anyone else. That's the kind of spirit we're actually looking for, isn't it?

Whatever the advantages of a competitive system—and in mortality, they are considerable—it is not the system that will exist in the next life. We can't imagine competition there, can we? So we have to be careful about the effects it has on us here. As President Kimball warned us, it may be our very prosperity that will bring us down—and cause us to worship our possessions as false gods.

No one has spoken more eloquently about our responsibilities to others than King Benjamin in the Book of Mormon. What he expressed so powerfully in his well-known sermon was that we owe everything we have to the Lord. This, he says, should lead us to humble ourselves and become "filled with the love of God" (Mosiah 4:12).

King Benjamin then talks about the way we should live. First, he tells us that we should look after our families, provide for them, make sure they never "go hungry, or naked." We should also teach our children to obey the laws of God and to not "quarrel one with another" or to serve Satan, the "enemy to all righteousness" (v. 14).

He then teaches us how we should treat others: ". . . ye will administer of your substance unto him that standeth in need; and ye will not suffer that the beggar putteth up his petition to you in vain, and turn him out to perish" (v.16).

We all understand that responsibility, but we also bristle a little sometimes at the idea that in giving to the poor, we might be helping people who are merely lazy—those hustlers we see on the streets who, we suspect, just might be making more money than we are. We hear all sorts of stories about those people and how they fake their need, use what we give them to buy alcohol and drugs, and on and on. We all have a long list of reasons to be skeptical, and no doubt, many of them are valid.

We also know what King Benjamin said about our resistance to giving to those who implore us: "Perhaps thou shalt say: The man has brought upon himself his misery; therefore I will stay my hand, and will not give unto him of my food, nor impart unto him of my substance that he may not suffer, for his punishments are just—But I say unto you, O man, whosoever doeth this the same hath great cause to repent; and except he repenteth of that which he hath done he perisheth forever, and hath no interest in the kingdom of God" (vv. 17–18).

Explaining his logic, Benjamin goes on: "For behold, are we not all beggars? Do we not all depend upon the same Being, even God, for all the substance which we have, for both food and raiment, and for gold, and for silver, and for all the riches which we have of every kind?" (v. 19).

I've been involved in some heartfelt and thoughtful discussions in priesthood and Sunday School classes about these passages. They do leave us in something of a quandary. Are we obligated to give to every beggar who ever approaches us? Was King Benjamin talking about the deserving poor, not con artists? But when I start down that road, I feel his words: "Perhaps thou shalt say: The man has brought upon himself his misery. . . ." I fear that that's exactly the argument I'm making. And then I wonder if I'll "perish" for my attitude.

What I know is that Christ taught many times that we have responsibility for each other and that we should not turn our backs on those who hunger. This is exactly where pure capitalism and pure Christianity meet head-on. If we think of our fellow humans as competitors for scarce resources, we may conclude that we owe them nothing. The challenge, I think, is to provide for our families but then look about us to help those who suffer—and there are many ways to suffer. Often such souls need our time more than our money.

Elder Alexander B. Morrison, a truly compassionate man, offered some guidance about how we might think about the dilemma we sometimes face:

> Caring for the poor in the Lord's way is not an easy thing to do; achieving the necessary balance between giving too much and

giving too little is one of the most difficult tasks priesthood leaders and others have to carry out. Each situation is different, requiring its own solution. All the poor are not the same. . . . Some are poor in economic terms; others are poor in spirit, depressed, disheartened, burdened with cares and sorrow, perhaps disabled. Among them are the aged, the widow, the single mother. All need compassion; all merit our concern. [*Visions of Zion* (Salt Lake City: Deseret Book Company, 1993), 107]

Church leaders have long warned us about the dangers of putting ourselves first. We often quote Elder J. Golden Kimball, but usually only for his wry humor. He also had serious things to say. He described society, as he saw it in 1934, during the Great Depression. He worried, among other things, about the "modern conception of time," which ". . . so completely fills our days with one pressing engagement after another." He saw people: " . . . running hither and thither, until we have little or no time to minister to the needy, the hungry, the naked, the disconsolate ones who are ever with us. It would almost seem that materialism and selfishness and greed have nearly driven out of us that Christlike spirit" (in Conference Report, April 1934, 32).

Elder Morrison described the attitude we can all work toward:

> As we develop compassion, the scales of indifference, self-righteousness, and selfishness fall from our eyes. We see and feel— perhaps for the first time—the suffering of others. We weep with them and for them. We weep, too, for our own weaknesses and imperfections. We reach out to help the less fortunate as best we can. We think less of ourselves and more of others. We set different priorities, eschewing the tawdry materialism that has claimed so much of our attention heretofore. We set aside "our consuming selfishness," our "love for comfort and ease." [*Visions of Zion*, 28–29]

If we remember that all we have, we owe to the Lord, we should also remember his admonitions about how we use our wealth. If we fail to impart our substance, and instead spend every penny of our money on ourselves, we're missing the point of Christ's teachings. King Benjamin recognized that some had so little that they couldn't give, but he advised them to say in their hearts, "I give not because I have not, but if I had I would give" (v. 24). Most of us have times when we can help others and other times when we need help, but our hearts can be right in either circumstance, and we can feel the connectedness that Christ wanted us to feel, one to another.

King Benjamin does give us one bit of guidance as we decide how much we can do for others. In verse 27, he says, "And see that all these things are done in wisdom and order; for it is not requisite that a man should run faster than he has strength." Clearly, no one person can solve all the inequities of this world, but just as clearly, to look at our fellow beings as drudges, out to get their hands into our pockets, goes against everything we are taught.

We learn in the scriptures that whenever a truly godly society has existed, such as during the years that followed Christ's visit to the new world, the people, moved by the Holy Spirit, have lived in peace and equality. We read in 4 Nephi 1:2–3:

> And it came to pass in the thirty and sixth year, the people were all converted unto the Lord, upon all the face of the land, both Nephites and Lamanites, and there were no contentions and disputations among them, and every man did deal justly one with another.
>
> And they had all things in common among them; therefore there were not rich or poor, bond and free, but they were all made free, and partakers of the heavenly gift.

Maybe it's too much to hope for, that our wards and communities would be holy places where all thought of competition would end. But it's the ideal Christ sets before us. "No rich or poor" certainly refers to relative wealth, but doesn't it mean much more than that? The ideal is mutual love and respect and a fundamental eagerness to support one another.

President Hinckley reminds us that we are to strive for that same mind-set in our day and prescribes how we can obtain it:

> If we are to build that Zion of which the prophets have spoken and of which the Lord has given mighty promise, we must set aside our consuming selfishness. We must rise above our love for comfort and ease, and in the very process of effort and struggle, even in our extremity, we shall become better acquainted with our God. ["Our Mission of Saving," *Ensign*, November 1991, 59]

I started this chapter by raising questions about teaching our children to pursue their dreams. What would life be like if we didn't have hopes and dreams? But I think we need to be careful about allowing the world to define our goals. Our heroes tend to be "winners": superstars and billionaires, sports stars and entertainers. Our admiration for so-called high achievers can imply that humble people, living worthy lives, are not as important. If we let our society tell us who is important, we'll fail to give credit to the person who quietly offers service in our communities; the woman who blesses others with her faith and optimism; the man who always shows up for welfare projects; the teenager who befriends someone others ignore.

So should we teach our children, "You've gotta have a dream"? I have no problem with doing that as long as we're clear about what we mean. I have a friend who wanted to be an artist, a painter. That was his dream, the only thing he'd ever wanted to be. He struggled for quite some time, bringing in little income and testing his faith in his own talent. But he developed his skills, gradually sold more of his work, and now he's become well-known. Through all this, he's remained well-grounded. He's a likeable, down-to-earth man with a good family. His paintings always depict the things he believes. He serves in his ward and in his community, and he never seems impressed with himself.

I'd call that something worth dreaming about.

I'd call him a great success.

But what if his dream hadn't worked out, and he'd "only" had a good family and served in his ward and community? Would the Lord think less of him? No. Would we? I hope not.

What worries me is that some young people set achieving fame as a goal—and what an empty goal that is. Look at some of our young "stars" these days, famous for being famous, living lives of corruption, reveling not in accomplishment but in the adulation of the fans who can't seem to get enough of them. In the hope of becoming great athletes or famous performers, some people are willing to give up everything else. Sometimes it's their parents who push them and distort their lives into narrow, self-centered, almost fanatic pursuits.

At times we see young people so bent on winning an Olympic medal, they practice all day every day and sacrifice much of what I would call "life." When they win, they often say, "I guess it hasn't sunk in yet," as though they wonder why they are not as ecstatic as they imagined they would be. Or they say, "It doesn't get any better than this," and I can only think, *Oh, but it ought to.* Don't tell me that devoting your entire youth to winning a hunk of metal is the best that life has to offer. It is a great achievement, but its value must be measured, at least in part, by what they gave up to reach it.

So, yes, let's dream our dreams and teach our kids to do the same, but let's see the whole picture. Maybe if we quit pushing so hard for attention, for status, for widgets, we would actually enjoy life much more. We all know the truth: we're happier when we're serving, not when we're insanely busy chasing after those phantoms we already know we "can't take with us."

We know this stuff, but we let ourselves get confused. And the question is, what can we do to keep our priorities clear? In the final two chapters in this book, I'm going to address some specific—and I hope, practical—ways to find the peace we're looking for, but for right now I think it might be worth taking some time to look closely at our lives and what we're doing with them. I recommend you consider one simple scripture. Nephi taught his people: "But the laborer in Zion shall labor for Zion; for if they labor for money they shall perish" (2 Nephi 26:31).

That's an interesting statement, isn't it? So I ask you—and me—what are we working for? Spend some time thinking about Nephi's words, maybe discussing them with your family. Before we can start in a new direction, we have to recognize where we're standing. There are a lot of roads extending out from the intersection we're facing, all calling for our attention, but the nice thing is, the right choice is the simple one. It's straight, though admittedly slightly uphill, and the going is easier when we drop most of the world's weight off our shoulders.

CHAPTER 3

Following Christ

WHEN I WAS A MISSIONARY, back in the early 1960s, I found a technique that I considered effective for teaching the Word of Wisdom. To encourage investigators to give up smoking I would ask them whether they could imagine Jesus smoking a cigarette. That image was bothersome to them, and it helped convince some people that the Word of Wisdom had a spiritual side, not just a health implication.

But I came to wonder about my own reasoning. The truth is, it's hard for most of us to imagine Christ doing much of anything that is modern and "everyday." We keep Him in our heads as an abstraction. From paintings and movies we've acquired a concept of His appearance that may or may not have much to do with what He really looked like. We see Him, in our minds, always moving gracefully, even slowly. He touches softly, speaks quietly, teaches gentle sermons. We do know that He overturned the tables in the courtyard of the temple and drove out the money changers, and we know that He could raise His voice in crying repentance, but still, we see Him mostly in pale robes, His eyes full of love, and not seeming very much like most of the people we know.

It's offensive to imagine Christ smoking, of course, but it's also hard to picture Him driving a car, riding on a roller coaster, or eating a hamburger. It's just hard for us to think of Him living in our time, and that brings on the other problem: It's hard to imagine what He would do in certain circumstances that we have to deal with.

When we seek the simple, straight path of following Christ, part of the difficulty is figuring out how to apply Christ's teaching to our twenty-first-century lives. I think that's another contributing factor to our confusion—another reason we let ourselves get lost. It seems as though the path will be easy to recognize—and ultimately, it is—but we need to keep our eyes on the path itself and not on all the bad road signs someone has stuck in our way.

Latter-day Saints have developed what you might call a "standard response" to many of the events of life. It's not necessarily what Christ would do, but it's a kind of shorthand way of knowing what's right and wrong in our own culture (notice that I didn't say, "in our own theology"). For instance, what do we do if people in our ward go through a family crisis?

We take food to them, of course.

If a baby is born, we take food.

If someone gets sick, we take food.

And when death comes, the Relief Society serves a meal after the funeral. And what do we serve? Ham and "funeral potatoes." Who doesn't know that?

Not that there's anything wrong with any of that, of course; I'm only saying that we learn a set of behaviors for certain situations, but we haven't even thought about many others. I notice, for instance, that some Church members believe it's bad to watch television on Sundays and others don't have a problem with it. Still, it's one of those things we don't say too much about, and on Super Bowl Sunday we don't admit our plans for that evening (but plenty of people seem to know all about the game the next day).

So is there a right answer—an official doctrine—on the question, or are we actually expected to think about it for ourselves? What a scary thought!

Lately, I've been posing for myself some ethical questions—ones I don't hear mentioned in church very often.

I attended an event at the Marriott Center on the Brigham Young University campus a few years back. President Gordon B. Hinckley was the final speaker. At the end, he admonished those of us who attended to be careful and courteous in our driving as we left the parking lot. The thought hit me in a way that it never had before that there might be a way that Christ would want us to drive.

Ever thought about that?

I've never heard the subject come up in a sacrament meeting talk, but we always hear the admonition at the end of general conference to be courteous as we drive home. There must be a reason for the suggestion.

When I got in my car that day, after having taken President Hinckley's word seriously, I realized that I sometimes change personalities when I leave a meeting like that, and suddenly my aggressive side appears. I'll have to admit, I'm a Type A personality, and it's not easy for me to deal with long delays in a crowded parking lot. But on that day, I told myself, I needed to drive courteously—as the prophet had asked us to do.

I was being patient, and most people were politely taking turns, when I saw a man take a hard left in his four-wheel-drive truck and climb over a curb and across a lawn. He might have taken out a few sprinkler heads and made tire trenches in the grass, but he got out of the parking lot a few minutes faster than he would have, had he waited. Now I know that sounds really crass of him, but I think it's one of those areas where Latter-day Saints have never established an exact set of standards. How should a "good Mormon" behave behind the wheel of a vehicle—especially with six, tired, cranky kids in the back?

My observation is that Latter-day Saints drive

about like everyone else. But why? And I'm asking seriously. Shouldn't the spirit of Christ's doctrines influence *everything* we do? Shouldn't we possess certain attitudes and behavioral patterns that would apply naturally to our choices in the practical world—at least the ones that affect how we treat other people? But when we get into a car, we think mostly about "getting there," and we're in a hurry. We wrap all that steel around us, and we assume a new mentality: now it's time to look out for myself. "I've got the biggest SUV on the road, and my kid is late for soccer practice."

One day I was driving on a quiet Provo street and I was in a hurry, as I always seem to be, and in front of me was an older woman going twenty miles an hour in a thirty-five-mile-per-hour zone. I was mumbling, trying not to get too out of sorts (which means, not screaming at her), when I realized she was a sister in my ward . . . *and I was her bishop!*

Funny how fast my attitude changed.

"Be careful, Sister; don't go too fast." I was not even sure she ought to be driving at her age, and I hoped everyone would be patient with her.

Suddenly I was not only following a sister I loved; I was also following Christ. Since that time, I've come to believe that I should notice a person trying to merge from an on-ramp, consider how I've felt in the same situation, and make way for that car—no, the *person* in that car—even though the law says I have the right of

44

way. I see many situations where I can stop and let someone make a left-hand turn in front of me when I might just as easily move ahead and let the person wait.

In fact, I have this idea that every time I let someone in or let someone turn in front of me, that that driver is going to do the same thing at some other intersection for someone else and that the whole world is going to become less aggressive and more cooperative. If we were to make this kind of driving habitual, wouldn't everyone feel happier, gentler, and less frenzied? And perhaps the Lord would be with us as we drive.

Well . . . anyway . . . it's nice to think so.

But we certainly won't change until we think about what we're doing and ask ourselves what's right. I think the world would be vastly improved if all of us who want to follow Christ would notice that driving has as much to do with living the gospel as keeping the Word of Wisdom, avoiding shopping on Sunday, or serving funeral potatoes to the bereaved.

For some reason, driving brings out a competitive spirit in us. We would never elbow someone out of the way so that we could move up in a line at the grocery store, but driving opens up the possibility of a kind of non-contact bullying behavior. Drivers who dare push hard enough can usually make others back off. And we don't mind honking at some "idiot" we would never insult face-to-face.

One morning I was trying to find a parking place at BYU. I spotted an open space one row over. I sped up and looped into that row just as another professor came barreling in the opposite direction. Because I'd been talking to myself about driving politely, I realized this was "one of those times" to give way. He turned into the parking spot, only to see that the space in front of him was also open. He pulled all the way through and left a space for me. I pulled in and we both got out of our cars. He smiled, rather sheepishly, and said, "I'm sure glad there were two spots—or I would have felt bad about beating you out."

What had happened, of course, was that we had had to look one another in the face, and now we were two people, relating as people, and not just two cars jockeying for position. But I'm going to admit something here: I really enjoyed being the one who had been polite. (The trouble is, now I've lost my reward by being so prideful about it.)

Or . . . maybe there's another way to look at it. It *does* feel good to do the right thing—even if I'd had to go park clear up by the Marriott Center.

Unless I was running late, of course.

But the way we drive is merely an example. So much of this has to do with being aware of how our simple actions affect other lives. Have you ever walked down a hallway and come to a clog where people have stopped to talk? You wait for a few seconds and they don't seem to notice you. They're so busy with their chatter that they're oblivious to your delay. That's my word for it: *oblivious.* I see it everywhere. And I find it *very* annoying.

I also find that sometimes I see a friend and I stop to chat, and *I* don't notice that I'm blocking the way of others. Oblivious.

You get my point.

There are so many examples. Have you ever noticed how many people stand in the aisle on airplanes while they put their carry-on luggage in the overhead? If they would step in between the seats, others could get by. I've noticed that and I try never to block people in that circumstance. I think that's what we should do: notice the things that bother us and learn from them. But. . . Eventually all the passengers make their way onto the airplane, and then we usually sit and wait a long time anyway. I should worry more about helping that five-foot-two woman with the hundred-pound carry-on—and stop fussing so much about getting myself seated.

By the way, why do people bring on those huge bags when they're supposed to check them? It just drives me . . . well, never mind. (But the next time I find a parking stall at the grocery store, only to find that someone has left a shopping cart in the middle of it . . . never mind that one, too.)

Contrary to what our religion requires of us, I think we sometimes give ourselves permission to be cranky with people. Let's say something goes wrong with that spectacular widget you bought. It's okay to be rude and loud when you complain over the phone or take the product back. Right?

It must be. I've done it.

Just as a car can make us feel anonymous and can dehumanize the other drivers on the road, so also can a telephone, e-mail, or even just a stranger on the other side of a desk (especially after a wait in a long line).

There are so many good reasons to be rude— apparently. I've seen active Latter-day Saints, good people, stand up in city council or school board meetings and *attack* other good people, directing ugly, insensitive accusations at them. The issue—the argument—has become more important than the *person* who holds a differing opinion. Read the letters to the editor in any newspaper, or listen to radio talk shows. Hateful statements about politics and about civic matters—and about people—are so commonplace, it's what we've come to expect. Some comedians seem to think the best humor should always demean someone. And intolerance can always be justified by saying, "I suppose I'm not being politically correct, but . . ."

How often have our Church leaders urged us to use civil, polite discourse, to respect others' opinions? Sometimes, in the name of righteousness, we actually become self-righteous and tactless.

And doesn't the matter go even deeper than that? I think we should be tactful, but don't we need to change our hearts as much as our words? On the day of the 9/11 terrorist attack, a devotional was scheduled at BYU. Elder Merrill J. Bateman, then president of the university, spoke to the campus community. He imparted good wisdom, but one thing he said took my breath away. He advised the students to pray for the victims, but also to pray for the misguided people who had carried out the attack. Not many of us felt ready to pray for the terrorists that morning, but he clearly wasn't just saying words. He meant it. And I sat there with tears in my eyes, thinking, "That's exactly what Christ would have us do."

I think many of us experience times when we just don't want to apply the maxim "follow Christ" to a particular part of our lives. And sometimes it's a very little thing that will throw us off. Here's an example. I'm at a grocery store. I assess the lines, try to pick the one that's likely to move fastest. (Time spent standing in line is perhaps the most painful period of a Type A Personality's life.) So I pick my line carefully, move up, and then realize that the sweet little lady with just a few items to purchase doesn't know about debit cards.

After the clerk says, "That will be $14.68," she *starts* to look for her checkbook.

Someone needs to tell her! *Nobody* uses checks anymore.

But she finds her checkbook after a long search (tucked in the bottom of her ample purse), and then she begins the tedious process of writing out "Day's Market," "fourteen and 68/00," and she signs her name as though she's practicing her penmanship.

By then, I'm shaking all over. And I'm thinking thoughts about this dear woman that no decent human ought to think about anyone, let alone about an aged Heber City woman who's probably my sister in the gospel.

I'm exaggerating a little, but I do find that lots of people frustrate me. And it's not my fault; it's theirs. They make me wait; they do things *the wrong way;* they don't know that they need to be in a hurry, the way normal people are.

But what would Christ do if He got stuck in a line at Day's Market and He had lots of errands to run and things to do? Here's my guess, or actually, it's what I *know* I ought to do. I ought to say to myself, "If my mother were still alive, she would be like that woman." In Mom's case, she would be counting out the exact change, digging one coin at a time from her coin purse, and if I were with her, I'd be smiling as I watched her. Because she's my mom.

Well, the lady in Day's Market is someone's mom. She's a nice woman, and she's getting older. And by the way, so am I. It won't be long until I'll be doing something just as slowly, and I'll be causing people to shake their heads at me. I should think about all that. I should think how much I'd love to see my mother, and I should treat the woman the way I'd like someone to treat Mom. "It's a beautiful day, isn't it?" I should say to her, and chat with her as we stand in line.

I should slow down. What is my rush to get through that line anyway? I should go out of my way to meet people, find out about their lives, swap a few stories, enjoy my day and enhance theirs.

Maybe the problem is, you're too much like me. We're all running too fast, trying to get somewhere whether we need to get there or not, and we're so focused on ourselves that someone moving at a reasonable pace becomes an offense to us.

Or maybe I'm the only one who acts that way. All I know is that I need to love that nice woman, and on my best days, I do.

So much of doing the right thing comes down to attitude—how we think about others, ourselves, relationships, and true religion. If we center our thoughts on *ourselves*, ask how everything affects *us*, we feel judgmental and impatient. It's that spirit of competition that loves to place one person above another mentally.

We feel superior, and that means we just won some sort of game we're playing in our minds.

All this makes so much sense to me in the abstract, but it's difficult to practice. And one of the reasons for that is that we often take on the mannerisms of the environments we live and work in. The competitive spirit of many workplaces can cancel, every Monday morning, what we've felt right about in church on Sunday. I'm convinced that making our careers and our faith mesh is one of the hardest jobs we'll face on this earth because both consume so much of our time, attention, and energy. The only sure thing is that we won't get the job done if we use one value system at work and try to switch to another each night when we come home.

Each vocation is different, but I do believe we have to ask ourselves every day how a Christian goes about our particular kind of work. There may be times when an action costs us a little money, or when helping an employee or fellow worker takes some time we didn't think we had. There are all kinds of situations in which we can bring kindness and consideration to our places of employment.

If we go to work and take on standards that are in subtle ways contradictory to the gospel, and justify our behavior as "the way things are done in this business," we lose more than we may recognize. Let's say that we advertise our product or service, and advertising always employs a certain amount of hype, doesn't it? But when does hype become a lie, and at what point are we changed into liars in order to make a buck? There are lots of people running around selling things, making promises. Some of them are us. And some of us need to worry about facing the Lord.

When I was in college I worked in a clothing store. I remember a man coming in and trying on a suit. It didn't fit quite right, but I really wanted to make the sale. I kept telling him that the tailor could surely make things right, and I actually did believe that was true. So I asked my boss, the store owner, to come over and help me, and I figured he'd close the deal. Instead, he told the customer, "I'd love to sell you this suit, but I just don't think you'd ever be happy with it." Then he explained how drastic the alterations would have to be. The man didn't buy a suit that day, but he remained a loyal customer. And I learned respect for my boss, who was a local Church leader and an honest man.

I think we each have to ask ourselves what is ethical and right within the context of our own vocations. And we all need to ask ourselves how we can put to use whatever measure of talent the Lord has given us. In every line of work there are ethical considerations, and there are also opportunities to treat coworkers and "competitors" with respect and kindness.

Is it possible to take pleasure in someone else's success? We'd like to think so. But what if the guy down the hallway gets the promotion *I* deserved? Can I congratulate the one who got the job—and mean it? All kinds of factors enter into the boss's decision—favoritism, perhaps, or flashy demeanor, whatever—but the boss did choose her, and not me. And the boss has reasons. Maybe I don't have to like the situation, but can I deal with it and let it go, or will I let it fester and build up resentment?

Most of our confusion about ethics is brought on by the competitive atmosphere we live in. We actually know the answers to most of the questions that come up. Since childhood we've known that we should "keep the commandments." But many of the commandments are about *not* doing certain things. Christ asks us to look more deeply into our behavior. He asks us to consider our actions and attitudes in light of how they affect those around us.

At our house we feed hummingbirds. We have two big containers with four little fake-flower feeders on each one. So eight hummingbirds can feed at the same time. There are times when we have ten or fifteen hummingbirds out there, and it's easy to see how the birds could feel competitive: limited resources, lots of little tummies to fill. But what makes me laugh is that two hummingbirds will fight over the eight spigots just as vigorously as ten will. One will be feeding when another appears at the *second* container—and the first one will chase off the new guy. Those little birds just can't get it through their heads that there's plenty of nectar for everyone. And there's something they don't know: there's more where that came from. I'm going to keep refilling those containers until the birds leave for the south, come fall.

Are we like that? Are we trying to gather in all the money, or attention, or prestige, or even love (love of God, love of others), as though we're fighting for a limited resource that might run out at any time? Some kinds of resources do become scarce, but the ones that matter do not. Our jobs are inevitably competitive, but that doesn't change our ultimate goal. If, when we end our careers, we have been successful in business but disabled as followers of Christ, we would have been better off not to have earned that corner office with a view. It's possible to have both, I know; I've seen it done many times. But the dangers and temptations are great and they vary from one vocation to another.

So what is this competitive spirit all about? Where does it come from? Isn't it, really, based on envy? We seem to feel that when others get what they work for, they somehow take it away from us. Elder Jeffrey R. Holland, in one of his finest sermons, described the feelings of the "other prodigal," in the parable of the Prodigal Son. It was the dutiful son, the one who never left home, who was upset when his foolish and willful brother received so much love and attention. As Elder Holland taught us, "He [the dutiful brother] has yet to come to the compassion and mercy, the charitable breadth of vision to see that *this is not a rival returning*. It is his brother."

And then Elder Holland asks:

> Who is it that whispers so subtly in our ear that a gift given to another somehow diminishes the blessings we have received? Who makes us feel that if God is smiling on another, then He surely must somehow be frowning on us? You and I both know who does this—it is the father of all lies. It is Lucifer, our common enemy, whose cry down through the corridors of time is always and to everyone, "Give me thine honor." ["The Other Prodigal," *Ensign*, May 2002, 63; emphasis in the original]

Envy. Has there ever been a less satisfying impulse? Has there ever been a more common one? But as much as anything, it's what we have to overcome if we want to find peace in this life.

I keep saying that we need to think right. I know that the challenges are ultimately more spiritual than mental. But it's hard to pray for guidance if we can't even identify the path we want to walk. We need to know what we're trying to accomplish all the time, not only when we're in our church meetings. We can't tell ourselves we're trying to follow Christ on his path and then act like those envious hummingbirds and try to knock people down as we push our way forward. The idea of doing that seems absurd when we have Christ's example before us—but when we convert that path into a city street, we easily lose sight that Christ is still up ahead. We can follow Christ in a car—even in an SUV—and in line at a grocery store and at our jobs. But we may have to look about a little more to see the path when it's not quite so clearly marked.

Let me offer a little exercise that has helped me adjust my thinking. It's what I've been doing lately. Some Christians suggest that you ask, in every situation, "What would Jesus do?" That's probably okay, but as I said before, we have a hard time thinking about Christ living in our time. I would pose the question a little differently.

I'd ask, "How would I want to be treated?"

That's not very original, is it? I think we've heard that before. But apply it all day to all your interactions with others. Just try it for one full day, and really concentrate on it. Everyone seems to be walking around *annoyed* these days, bothered by all the *idiots* they have to deal with. But aren't we all someone else's idiot, sooner or later? So turn the situation around in your mind. If I cut someone off in traffic, wouldn't I want the offended driver to say, "I've done that myself," rather than to lean on the horn and signal that I'm number one (so to speak)?

Habits are hard to change, but I've been trying the last couple of years to think about people in reverse—putting myself in their places and they in mine—and it's actually had a positive effect. I'm still impatient, and my friends would probably be surprised to hear that I think I've changed, but I'm feeling different inside, and that's a start. Some days I actually find the path obvious—right before me.

CHAPTER 4

Seeing Clearly

I'VE TRIED TO MAKE MY CASE that a spirit of competitiveness is contrary to the Lord's desires for us. I believe it distorts our perspectives and causes us to establish false priorities and false values. What I want to do now is relate some personal experiences that have caused me to rethink my own life. I'm hoping that my process of realization might add some further light to what I've been saying.

A few years ago I made a discovery that caused me to reconsider many of my lifelong habits of mind. I had gone to see my family doctor, and he had some test results for me. He told me that my cholesterol was in good shape and congratulated me, and then he said, "But your PSA has gone up." It had jumped several points. He spent some time explaining what that might mean, and as I began to get the picture, I said, "Are you telling me I have prostate cancer?"

"I think you probably do," he told me, "but we

won't know for sure until you have a biopsy. We need to get that scheduled." Then he reassured me. If I did have cancer, we had probably caught it early, and if that were the case, I might need surgery, but once that was done, my chances of being cured were 90 percent or better.

Don't shut the book. This isn't one of those "savor every minute of your lives" sermons. I suppose that's a good thing to do, but it's not the point I'm about to make.

While driving home after my appointment, I tried to get used to the idea that I might have cancer. I waited for panic to set in, but I felt okay. We had probably caught it early, and "90 percent" sounded like good odds. I didn't like the idea of having surgery, but I figured I would deal with that if it came.

I thought about calling my wife, Kathy, but this was during the time she was serving in the general presidency of the Relief Society, and I knew she was at her Salt Lake City office, in a meeting. I decided not to call until I got home. So I left the clinic in Provo and drove up Provo Canyon to our home in Midway, Utah. Along the way—a trip of half an hour or so—I continued to measure my reaction, and I thought again about the idea that we had "probably" found my cancer early. But . . . what if we hadn't? I had actually been lax about going in for a physical, and maybe I'd allowed too much time between PSA tests. I also thought about the

90 percent. That left the other 10 percent. I didn't like the image that came to my mind: ten guys standing in a line, and one of them takes a bullet in the chest. I thought I might like to be standing in a little bigger crowd.

That's when it hit me. Maybe I would die.

You have to understand, I've known for a long time that I would die someday. But this was *real* death from a *real cause* we were talking about. There's the kind that's always been there, always will be—the abstract *idea* of death. And then there's *actual* death—the kind that ends your life.

So I thought about it, straight on. How did I feel about dying, say, in the next year or two? (I later learned that much can be done these days, and I didn't have to be quite so frightened—but I'd never had cancer before, so what did I know?) What I realized, clearly, was that I didn't want to die right away. That's not too surprising, I guess. But now you expect me to say that I immediately readjusted my priorities and began to "set things straight" with the Lord. Actually, I'm still sort of shocked at the thought that did go through my mind. It was: "But I still haven't written a great book."

That was something I'd started to dream about as a kid. The desire had been with me all my life. Still, I thought I'd grown up. I thought I'd readjusted my priorities. But there I was, still hoping to *prove myself.*

But prove myself to whom? I guess I was still hoping to be loved and respected by the lone and dreary world that I seem to love too much.

I reached Heber Valley and turned toward Midway. I decided I could probably reach Kathy by then, so I got out my cell phone and began to punch in the numbers (while driving, which will probably be illegal before much longer).

And that's when it hit me—bam—like a meteor slamming through the roof of my car and on into my brain. I was about to call my wife to tell her I probably had cancer and I was worrying about myself. I was wondering whether the world would forget me when I was gone . . . whether I had "made my mark" . . . or some such thing.

Do you know what I'm talking about? I was told when I was a kid to "think big," to "go for the top," to "hitch my wagon to a star," to "let nothing stand in my way." All those things we're probably telling our kids. And all my life, try as I may to think about the real purpose of life, I had developed the habit of finding my joy in the achievements that seemed to make me important in other people's eyes.

It hit me hard at that moment that I should have been thinking about *Kathy*. I should have been thinking about my kids and grandkids. I should have been thinking about the Lord. But I was still *competing*. I couldn't let go of the idea that I needed to be "some-body."

You're probably saying right now, "Okay. Got that. You've been telling us that for three chapters." But what I'm trying to say is that, sooner or later, we have to wake up. And it's really too bad if we have to wait until death is staring us in the face to say, "Wait a minute; I've been getting this whole thing wrong."

I'm not quite sure whether it's our minds or our hearts that have to be changed first—because the important change is in the heart—but for me, my refo-cusing process started in my head. I suddenly *saw* everything differently, *thought* differently. I realized that all my life Babylon had been teaching me to worry about the wrong things. It suddenly seemed possible that it was okay to "think small." Or maybe, to change what I thought "big" was. It's as though I turned the spy-glass around and the size of everything reversed. "Kindness" was suddenly huge and the victories and championships of the world looked like silly little games. (Maybe because most of them *are* games.)

But seeing that was only the bare beginning, and changing is, I've learned, surprisingly hard. Just when I think the picture is clear to me, the projector seems to slip out of focus. What I've been trying to do, though, is to look at myself more honestly than ever before, and try to understand what pushes me in the wrong direction. That process of self-discovery, in my opinion, can help us all.

As it turned out, I did have cancer. I had the surgery and I'm okay. My urologist tells me I will *not* die of prostate cancer. But I know this now: I *will* die of something. I may live another forty years—many do now—but I will finally die. But here's what I try to keep clear in my mind: At some point, I will have to stand before the Lord and account for myself. And I think life will look vastly different from that perspective. What matters so much here probably won't matter very much there. I have to keep that thought before me all the time if I want my vision to stay clear.

The Lord won't ask me whether I wrote a great book. But He *will* care whether I used a talent I received from Him, developed it, and used it well. In other words, I think the Lord will want to know whether I was willing to sell my soul to achieve my goals.

Elder Dallin H. Oaks expressed the idea this way:

> The Final Judgment is not just an evaluation of a sum total of good and evil acts—what we have *done*. It is an acknowledgment of the final effect of our acts and thoughts—what we have *become*. It is not enough for anyone just to go through the motions. The commandments, ordinances, and covenants of the gospel are not a list of deposits

required to be made in some heavenly account. The gospel of Jesus Christ is a plan that shows us how to become what our Heavenly Father desires us to become. ["The Challenge to Become," *Ensign*, November 2000, 32]

So how will that judgment take place? Will the Lord compare me to others and give me a percentile rating? Will He use a bell curve? Will He rate my fame or reputation? Surely it's nice to be "known for good" among our peers, but the fact is, we can look good to the world and not *be* very good. But the Lord knows our hearts. He understands our motivations. He'll know whether we really *are* good.

The Lord won't judge me, or you, merely by our actions—because we mess up too often. As Elder Oaks said, He'll judge the results we came up with. He'll know if we learned some patience even though impatience was a weakness of ours. He'll know if we softened ourselves enough to be less judgmental, more understanding. He'll notice if we learned to trust more in Him as our faith deepened. He'll recognize if eventually we didn't have to get knocked down before we became contrite, if we got some perspective, saw ourselves more clearly, and gave up some of our pride.

I think on that day we'll be wishing we had worried a lot less about winning and a lot more about giving, supporting, waiting patiently, and thinking good thoughts about those we love—and those we don't. And on that day, we'll wonder why we spent our whole lives trying to be "successful" in the world's eyes when such simple things could make us successful in His. It's what I see clearly now—that I worried way too much about proving myself to people and too little about proving myself to the Lord.

But here's the challenge: not just to get this idea in our heads, but to *keep* it there. And that's why I think it helps to stop and look back at our lives, to measure what it is we've been striving for and what matters most to us, and to determine whether we've kept our priorities straight.

I grew up wanting to be *somebody*—wanting to be "important." My first home was a trailer house on the poor side of Ogden, Utah. It wasn't one of those fancy double-wide mobile homes. It wasn't even as big as the little travel trailers you see on the highway. It was eight feet wide and sixteen feet long. (I've seen walk-in closets that big.) My mom and dad slept in a hide-a-bed, and my brother and I slept on a roll-away. When both beds were opened, they filled the whole trailer. We used a bathroom in the trailer court "wash house." It wasn't exactly an outhouse, but we certainly had to leave our house to get there. We had no refrigerator; instead, we kept an icebox outside the trailer and an "ice man" used to come around and drop a block of ice in it once a week, or whatever his schedule was.

This was during World War II, and my dad was working for the railroad while my parents saved their money so we could buy a house. When I was five we moved into a sort of "fourplex," except that it was really a big old house divided into four living areas. We shared a bathroom with another family. My older brother and I slept on the roll-away bed again, which was now placed in the kitchen. Mom and Dad still used the hide-a-bed, now located in the living room. Those two rooms were the entire apartment.

Finally, when I was ten, we bought a house. It cost $5,700. (Notice, that's fifty-seven *hundred*, not thousand.) It was below Washington Boulevard, a sort of dividing line in Ogden, where prestige was measured by how far up the mountain a person lived—and we were closer to the railroad tracks.

As I got older I began to realize that I was poor. I guess it was that—knowing that I lived in the wrong part of town and knowing what a humble house we had—that caused me to feel I needed to "make something of myself." By the time I reached junior high, I had figured out how I was going to do that. Teachers, by then, had started to tell me that I was a good writer—and I loved to read. So that's what I thought I'd like to do: write books. I imagined a day when a title page would have my name on it, and it seemed some sort of ultimate. I guess I thought I would be rich and famous if I published a book. I suspected, at the very least, that people would look up to me and respect me. I would be an *author,* and that was *important.*

Most kids give up their childhood dreams, but I didn't. I wrote a great deal in high school, and I took an excellent creative writing class at Ogden High. I started a novel when I was a senior. It was never published, but I kept writing in college. I majored in English and took all the creative writing classes I could. I did my master's degree in creative writing, and then I went on in literature to get a Ph.D. at the University of Washington in Seattle. My dad could barely read, and I ended up with a doctorate in literature—because I was *driven* to publish books.

That's good, isn't it?

Yes. In a lot of ways it is.

I wrote another book in college that was never published, and then I did a third one during my first years as an English professor at a university in Missouri. That book was later published, but it was turned down at first. That didn't stop me. I wrote a fourth book, and that one was finally accepted by a publisher.

On the day I received the good news, I literally leaped in the air I was so excited. I went searching for my wife to tell her what had happened. Our family went out to dinner that night, to celebrate. I was thirty-four by then, and Kathy and I had three children. I had pursued my dream for most of my life, and now it had happened. I was an author.

So why didn't the euphoria last very long? The book came out, sales were decent, and I was pleased. But I didn't feel transformed. What I had published was a children's novel, and some people asked me, "Would you like to write for adults someday?" That made the accomplishment seem trivial, I suppose, but beyond that, I simply didn't feel changed. Clearly, I was not yet *important.*

So I wrote more books. I hoped for bigger sales, for starred reviews, for paperback reprints, for name recognition. Eventually, all of those things came in various degrees, but there were always other writers who sold more copies of their books, who won more awards, who were truly famous. In short, I've spent my life writing and publishing, and I'm still the same guy I always was. I'm still that kid from Grant Avenue in Ogden, Utah.

Is any of this sounding familiar? Don't most of us dream our dreams and create great expectations about our lives, and don't most of us carry our self-doubts into adulthood and old age? And don't we also live dualistic lives? We know the Lord's goal for us: to learn from mortality and to become more like Him. We also know that a lot of what occupies us really isn't as important as our spiritual goals. But we're often drawn to our worldly pursuits more than to eternal growth.

Part of the reason may be that the payoff appears more immediate, more enticing. Being kind and considerate is nice, but making money, building a reputation, becoming "prominent"—all those things are a lot more exciting and more satisfying to our egos.

Here's the dilemma: We feel guilty that we aren't putting first things first—if and when we stop to think about it—but we still devote most of our time and effort to the things we know are transitory. And then, after giving our hearts to those pursuits, they end up giving us little return for all the work we put into them. The acquisition of money and worldly prestige are astoundingly disappointing results of our efforts.

I see so much wasted effort in our world: people setting goals and going after them as though the achievement is all-important. Someone decides to run all the way across America, backwards, while juggling . . . or some such thing. No doubt, that takes stamina and concentration, which are good traits. But, really, does the accomplishment itself matter?

"No one else has ever done it," the backward-running juggler says. "True, a couple of people did it forwards, but *backwards?*"

Strange. What is this thing we have about doing something *no one* has ever done? Do we really think that it lifts us above the pack? Is it a pathetic search for immortality?

I hear about these kinds of odd achievements all

the time, and I wonder, are we trying to invent meaning in our lives? Are we trying to give significance to lives that feel empty?

Maybe backwards juggle-running seems stupid to you, but what's your passion? Most of us have one—or more. We're told that mountain climbers do what they do "because it's there." I've always liked that. I like the idea that humans see a challenge and can't resist pursuing it. It's our nature to explore, to seek new frontiers. Challenges make life exciting and interesting, and we learn lessons from achieving them. But distortion of values sneaks in subtly when we give our hearts over to our worldly goals.

I once prayed that I would never have to be a bishop.

Actually, not just once. Many times.

And why? Because my writing was more important to me.

I had served as a counselor several times, and at that moment I was serving as a first counselor. I knew our bishop was due to be released, and I feared what might happen. I asked the Lord not to call me, and He didn't. But it was a bad year. Lots of things went wrong, and I needed the Lord. So I knelt, finally, and night after night, said I was sorry. I would commit myself. I would do whatever the Lord asked of me. I would finally put first things first.

To tell the truth, I thought I was safe. We had a new bishop, and I was still first counselor.

And then the bishop, less than a year after being called, was called into our stake presidency. And I was called to be bishop. I accepted and then went home and cried. I was scared I wouldn't be good at the administrative part of the calling, but I was also scared what might happen when the phone rang all day while I was writing.

As it turned out, I did some of the best writing of my life during that time, but that's not the point I'm trying to make. My point would be the same if my writing had gone badly. The danger is, we create goals, or we strive for achievements, and they become all-consuming. It's as though we say, "Yes, I'm all for living the commandments, having a nice family, being a good human being, and serving my fellowman—but now, give me something with some *real* meaning."

I almost missed the chance to serve as bishop—one of the most important experiences of my life—because I wanted to write that "great" book, and I feared serving the Lord might get in the way.

There it is, baldly stated, and I never would have expressed it that way at the time. But it's the truth.

I haven't given up my desire to write well, but I've changed my attitude about the relative importance of my career and my *life*.

The danger is not in doing what we do at a high

level; the danger is thinking that the things we do for a living or as an avocation are more important than the people around us, in thinking that we're better than others because we do something well, or in failing to recognize that spiritual skills need equal or greater attention.

I'm not ashamed of the desire I have to develop my talent. Inevitably, though, I end up comparing my work to that of other writers. Even that is not so bad when I have enough humility to accept that many others have greater talent. But it's a short step, once I start to compare, into the realms of envy and jealousy.

Some people seem to be able to compete in their careers the way they do at tennis or Monopoly. They play by the rules, play fair, and remain good-natured about it. Some business leaders try to be considerate of their employees, use their income to do good works— and all the rest. I know lots of LDS entrepreneurs and business managers who are noble and good, admired, and balanced in their lives. They leave work at quitting time and give their lives to their families and their church. They care about people and care about their communities, and they offer their valuable time to serve on community boards, coach in local leagues, and to serve in the Church. They do their best in their work, but they haven't lost track of what matters even more.

But it's not always easy to keep that balance. We

face hard choices, and we live with realities that sometimes steal away our youthful idealism. My son Tom
really wanted to be an actor. He also wanted to be a
good provider for his family, and he wanted to perform
in plays and films that wouldn't compromise his values.
He ended up giving up his acting career, at least for
now, to enter a more stable, predictable profession.
Some would say that he failed, that he didn't reach his
dream. I would say that in his particular case, he put
first things first.

And that's what I want to do. I want to get my priorities right, and I don't want to feel that doing so is a
constant struggle or a compromise. Latter-day Saints
often talk about "striving for perfection." I know that's a
good thing, but I don't want to fight for a little
progress and feel as though I'm swimming upstream
the whole way. I want to feel goodness inside me, filling me up. I not only want to stop being a jerk; I want
to discard my attraction for jerkiness. I want my
impulses to be pure, my faith consistent, and charity
my normal way of thinking and acting.

I want peace, not struggle.

I've met people who have progressed far beyond
me in this regard—people who consistently respond to
others with kindness and goodwill. I think it's something all of us can do, or at least it's something all of us
can move toward. We can come to a point in our lives
where goodness doesn't seem a stretch, that it actually

is our way of reacting to life. So much of that is steady improvement, not necessarily dramatic change. Elder Neal A. Maxwell wrote:

> Accumulating righteousness . . . may not immunize us, but it strengthens us, for we can respond out of reflex without reprocessing, again and again, the same tired, old temptations.

> There is a great safety . . . in the day-to-day world, in our being careful about maintaining our spiritual environment and in doing our duties. It is not just a question of being kept too busy to sin grievously, though that is preferred to excessive leisure, but of our being freely and anxiously engaged because we are true believers. Therefore, the rejection of temptation by reflex is superior to agonizing any time— better to be practical than theatrical! [*Not Withstanding My Weakness*, Salt Lake City: Deseret Book, 1981, 88]

Progress is possible, and as Elder Maxwell taught us, it can be steady and consistent. I suspect that it need not feel like "striving." I know it seems as though we're not getting anywhere at times, but this much I'm sure of: We won't make *any* progress if we spend our lives with all the wrong goals in our heads. Making money has its place, kept in bounds. Being known is not necessarily a bad thing. Being assessed by others as important is their choice, not ours, but there's nothing exactly wrong with that. Still, if we devote our lives to becoming important to the world, we may be unfortunate enough to reach our goal. If we spend our lives learning meekness, and achieve nothing more, we've not only changed ourselves—denied our greed—but we've made this world slightly better.

At the end of these chapters, I've been inviting you to do some self-assessment. I'm thinking now that it might be good for you to tell yourself your own story—maybe write it down. How did you become the person you are? What are your passions, and where did they come from? Are some of your personal traits actually the product of insecurity, a need to please, or a fear of "failure"? What matters most to you? Whom are you trying to impress? Could you actually make your life simpler and happier—and more in line with the gospel—by letting go of the need to appear "successful" to the world?

Supposing you only had a short time to live? What would matter then?

I know, that's an old question, a kind of game we play sometimes. But think about that *real* death I talked about, not the one that exists only as an idea. What kind of person have you *become* so far? And who would you like to be?

Be careful. You can pile guilt on your own head, and then you'll only want to run from the question. That's not the point. My guess is, you're like most of us: you're a good person and you know what matters most, but you let the world influence you more than you want it to. So I'm not asking you what more you need to do; I'm asking you to *do* less. I'm asking you if there are any useless desires and drives you could set aside—and be happier for doing so.

CHAPTER 5

Looking Good vs. Being Good

EVERY TIME I PLAY GOLF I learn the same thing. The pace of my swing is too quick. I need to slow down and make a smooth stroke. So why don't I fix the problem the next time I play? I have no idea. It's as though I can't make the change and make it permanent. Do you find life like that? Do you have to learn and relearn, and then learn it all again?

Part of the problem, I think, is that the complexity of life and the demands upon us tend to break our concentration, scatter our focus on what we're trying to do. Elder M. Russell Ballard, in a talk at general conference in the fall of 2006, advised us that we should stop making life so complicated. He told us to "be wise," to cut out needless frills ("O Be Wise," *Ensign*, November 2006, 17). We all believed him, told each other how right he was, and then I slipped back into my routine of ever-escalating busyness, unsure what I could cut out. I suspect most of us did the same thing.

We say we want out of the "rat race," but in truth, don't we choose the intensity of our lives by multitasking, spreading ourselves too thin, filling our schedules too full—and then complaining about it? "Simplify!" is what we tell ourselves, and make a note in our planner to work on doing just that—as we rush to answer our cell phones and check our e-mails.

Elder Ballard also said in the same talk that we should never use guilt to motivate one another. I could hardly believe my ears! I agreed with him entirely, but guilt has always seemed the heavy grease that keeps the wagon wheel of the Church rolling. We use it to "encourage" people to home teach, to attend their meetings, to do their family history work, to attend the temple . . . and just about everything else. So why would he give us the advice to back off on using guilt?

Here's my opinion, based on my own experience. When people respond to guilt—especially guilt pressed on them by others—they often become passive-aggressive in their responses. They may do what they're asked to do, but they do it with a certain degree of veiled resentment. We all know that mood when we comply, outwardly, and at the same time remain unwilling to commit ourselves spiritually to what we feel pressured to do.

It's true that guilt can also result from the promptings of the Spirit. We simply feel wrong about the direction we're heading. It's what people call conscience and what we call the Light of Christ or the influence of the Holy Ghost. The problem is not with having an internal desire to improve; it's the sense we have that we're living up to someone else's expectations.

We long to find authenticity in our faith, purity in our motives, clarity in our purposes. But we know ourselves and feel the gap between the ideal and the actual in our inner life. I think we all suspect that if others could look inside our heads, they would be shocked by what they would find there. We'd like to think that we're not the only ones with such pettiness, greed, jealousy, and resentment in our minds, but who wants to admit his or her own impulses in the hope that others will fess up, too? So we play it safe. We present our best self to the world and live with the suspicion that we're worse than most others.

What I'm getting to is the idea that we all live with a gap between our public and private selves. But to move along this road I've been talking about—of following Christ instead of Babylon, of escaping the gamesmanship going on around us—one of the challenges is to integrate who we are with who we appear to be. I asked you to think about yourself, to identify your motivations, and to decide what needs to change. As we move in that direction, I think it's very important to discover in ourselves the contradictions that hold us back from an authentic religious life.

I think there are ways to get closer to the ideal—
to that place where our impulses are less polluted—but
some element of the "natural man" persists in us and
always will. And that means we live with that oldest of
all contradictions. Remember Paul's courageous con-
fession when he acknowledged: "For what I would, that
do I not; but what I hate, that do I" (Romans 7:15).

One of our painful secrets is that our families just
don't fit the description we hear of the perfect LDS
family. A mother loses her cool and finds herself
screaming threats at her kids, and then wonders what
the sisters in Relief Society would think of her. She's
talked to her friends and ward members enough to
know that others struggle the same way, but still . . .
when the visiting teachers arrive, she puts on the best
face she can. And she wonders whether they heard her
yelling just before the doorbell rang.

A father knows he's supposed to be the spiritual
leader in his home, but his work seems to fill his head.
He comes home stressed, with hours of paperwork still
ahead of him. When his wife asks him whether it isn't
time for him to call the family together for prayer, he
resents what seems a veiled accusation, and he snaps at
her. He realizes what he's done and apologizes, but he
feels as though he's following orders when he calls to
his children. His mind isn't on the prayer, and he's
annoyed that his teenaged daughter hasn't started her
homework when it's actually time to go to bed. He

chews her out and then goes back to his work. It's only when he gets in bed, very late, that he begins to feel regret for the spirit he's brought into his own home all evening.

I think most families function *in and around* their dysfunction. Kids fight with each other. Parents lose their patience. All the influences of a wicked world are intruding into our homes these days—electronically—and we're not immune to those forces. And there are deeper problems, too: the ones we talk to our bishops about and fear that anyone would ever know. I learned as a bishop that *all* families have problems, some of them fairly superficial and some profound, but no family is quite like that picture we all have in our minds of the perfect group gathered for home evening in a loving, sacred atmosphere.

I'm not saying that everything's wrong in our families. Far from it. We're simply not all we'd like to be. Because the bar we've set is so very high, we often feel as though we're leaping at the sky—and if we're not careful, discouragement sets in and adds to our stress and worry.

Here's one of the things that happens in the Church. The bishop starts to realize, from things he hears and sees, that far too many people are failing to hold family home evening regularly. (Maybe he's also aware of the problem because his own family has also been irregular about that lately.) He honestly believes that the members should be encouraged to do better, so he decides to make home evening the subject of a sacrament meeting. He thinks of one of his best-example families, the Christensens, and asks the whole family to speak and sing and generally demonstrate how "love at home" really works. (I'd have to check the records, but I think there are more Christensen families in the Church than Smiths or Johnsons or Joneses.)

Brother and Sister Christensen accept the invitation, but neither has the nerve to say, "Actually . . . lately . . . we've been busy on Mondays quite often . . . and . . . we haven't always been as regular about holding . . ." (Or in some cases the Christensens do fess up, and the bishop still extends the invitation, knowing full well he might have to go down a long list to find a family that lives up to the full ideal.) In any case, the Christensens agree, and they only have one Monday available before the talk, so on that Monday they make an all-out effort to hold a model home evening. They enjoy it, and it goes well, and that's what they talk about in sacrament meeting. They tell what it did for their family, and the whole family sings a beautiful hymn, with big sister, Heather, playing the piano. Then little Tanner, Tyler, McKenna, and Madison give excellent talks.

It's very inspiring and a lot of couples go home and talk about their need to do better, and there's a resurgence of home evenings around the ward. But at least three women "need to see" the bishop that week, and a dozen more feel the desire but don't call. And what's their problem? They are devastated by the guilt of knowing that their families are simply not as good as the Christensens, and never will be.

You notice that I said "three *women.*" I usually found, when I was bishop, that it was the women in the Church who worried most about such things. I'll leave it to others to decide what to make of that.

I don't think it would work to go the other way—and constantly confess our sins to each other. And it's true that we need an ideal to work toward. But if we think about it, we know that humans will always fall short of the ideal. There are also private matters that don't need to be announced to the congregation. But I do wish we wouldn't cover up quite so completely, that we wouldn't make other families feel like the only sinners in the ward.

At church we tell about the wonderful letter we got from our missionary son; we relate a "missionary opportunity" that came our way; we report our joy in finding a name we'd been seeking in our family history research. These are good things to do. The only problem is that when we hear of others' best moments, we tend to compare them to our own worst moments. We think of a son who decided not to go on a mission; we chide ourselves for not trying hard enough to do missionary work; we know we set up PAF on our computers and started to put in names—and didn't get very far.

Because we preach the gospel to the world, and because family life is such an emphasis in our church, we feel that we need to present our best face to all who meet us. Within the Church, we often portray, in various images, those wonderful families we long to be: all the kids excelling in every way, and all the marriages consistently blissful. We shine up our kids and march them to church, and we smile even if death threats had to be employed to get the teenagers up for a nine o'clock sacrament meeting.

There's nothing new about this. It's certainly not unique to Latter-day Saints. But maybe we have our special brand of this kind of . . . hypocrisy. Maybe that's too strong a word. But when Christ uses the word in the New Testament, it is translated from a Greek word that means "play acting." And there certainly is a danger when and if our religious devotion crosses a line and becomes more appearance than reality.

This divide in our lives—always wondering whether we're as righteous as others perceive us to be—can damage us over time. And we certainly can do damage when we make others feel that they just don't belong among such wonderful people. More than once I've seen individuals or whole families slip into inactivity because they've felt out of place among so many people they perceived to be better than themselves.

There's another problem—a much more significant one. If we concentrate so much on looking good, we can easily forget that the real job is to *be* good. We can warn our kids to straighten up in certain circumstances and not realize that we're teaching them to *appear* to be something they're not. They can come to think that an outward show of religion is enough. All children discover at some point that a lie can save them from punishment. What child hasn't said, "He started it," or, "I wasn't doing anything"? whether it's true or not. Parents try to make sure their kids don't get away with that kind of thing. "I *saw* you," we say. But if we allow them—even teach them—to use the same techniques outside our home, we convince them that they have to be good at looking good and then they'll be all right.

Rob, our younger son, was asked to be a leader for the eleven-year-old Boy Scouts. You need to know, Rob really liked Scouting when he was a deacon, but we had to twist his arm, almost literally, to get him to finish his Eagle before he turned eighteen. Now he's in his thirties, and he was dealing with young boys, trying to get them motivated about the program. He's the lease orthodox of our children, but not long after receiving his call, he started to complain to his mother and me. He would tell us, "The parents want their sons to get advancements, but they don't care whether they learn anything. They want me to pass the kids whether they've done the work or not."

His diagnosis, after a time, was that parents see the Eagle badge as part of what a "good Mormon boy" is supposed to achieve. There was a time, he argues, when the Eagle was hard to get, a really significant accomplishment, but now the kids just want to be passed off on their merit badges whether they've put out an effort or not—and their parents back them up. They want the badge; they don't care about the principles of Scouting and what it's all supposed to mean.

That may seem a harsh judgment, especially from someone who had to be cajoled into finishing up his own Eagle. The truth is, though, Rob liked the activities, liked what he learned about getting along in the woods, about nature. He still loves to camp and hike, and he didn't learn that from me. What has stuck in his head is the idea that it's more important to *earn* an Eagle than it is to merely *get* one.

Is it all part of a Latter-day Saint image? Our sons should receive the Duty to God and the Eagle awards and our daughters should receive their Young Women medallion. All our kids should also develop talents: play an instrument, play sports, or "achieve" in some way. They should get good grades, go to college, and go on missions. And they should marry in the temple, have a nice family, and teach *our* grandchildren to do the same.

There's not one thing wrong with that. Certainly, that's the pattern we want for our children. But I started with the word *image*. Is it an *image* or is it *life?*

Research has shown that the most significant characteristic in determining whether or not a young person will stay committed to the Church in adulthood is the practice of "personal worship." I didn't say that if they "read" the scriptures every day they will stay with the Church. It's *personal worship* that makes the difference. That means "praying," not "saying your prayers." That means having the faith to make a personal effort to know the truthfulness of the gospel and its restoration through the Prophet Joseph Smith. We can teach our children to pray and read the scriptures, but at some point those actions have to turn into individual worship, individual faith, an actual testimony.

We're always in danger of teaching children to go through the motions without ever letting the Spirit reach the core of their behavior. If we're not careful, we can teach them that a badge means something, when in fact, it's the work to get the badge that matters. And in the same way, we can teach them to dress a certain way, clean up a certain way, say the right things, give the right answers in Sunday School, and even go on a mission—without their ever internalizing the principles behind such behaviors.

Here's a favorite missionary story. We've all heard it. The missionaries meet a fellow who has long hair and a beard, tattoos, and earrings. The guy doesn't believe in anything. The missionaries teach him the lessons and he reads the Book of Mormon, quits smoking and drinking, and receives answers to his prayers. He joins the Church and becomes a new man. He cleans up and cuts his hair, and now he's elders quorum president.

A lot of things get mixed together in that story, but notice how the change in appearance almost seems more significant to us than the "coming to Christ" aspect of the conversion. It's as though we're saying, "Now he looks more like us, and that makes him one of us." I know that President Hinckley has talked to us about being clean and neat. He's recommended against tattoos and body piercing. No one could agree with that more than I do. And I also agree that changes in appearance do have significance. But don't we have to be careful not to communicate the idea that you become a Latter-day Saint when you take on a certain approved appearance, instead of when you have experienced a mighty change of heart and a spiritual rebirth?

It's not the most important point to be made here, but variety of appearance, of expression, of background, shouldn't frighten us. We should embrace it and enjoy it. We're a worldwide church, and our message shouldn't be that Africans and Asians and South Americans should join the Church and then work the rest of their lives to appear like North Americans—or even be exactly like people of other nations. The Church can handle the richness that comes with inclusion.

What is most important is to recognize that true followers of Christ *walk His path*. That doesn't mean that they take on His mannerisms. It means that they genuinely love, forgive, and practice what He teaches. I fear that some of us have a tendency to turn to our brothers and sisters for the example of how we should think about *everything*. I've noticed an almost frightening degree of sameness in us. We echo one another's opinions on almost every subject—politics, current events, and cultural values.

When Kathy and I lived in Missouri, a nice young woman joined the Church and started coming to our ward. She got up in testimony meeting the first two or three months and said how happy she was that she had "found Jesus." I could almost feel the members squirm. Something about her words made me a little nervous, too. But finally she got the idea. The conventional expression is: "I'm so grateful to have a testimony of Jesus Christ." Collective sigh. She was going to be all right.

I'll admit that the term "finding Jesus" carries with it some possible theological implications. It might be "born again" language, and that can influence the way a person thinks about conversion. But in this case, the young woman simply hadn't learned the lingo—to speak the way our lifelong members speak. We have our own language, as we all know, and that's true of any culture, but language has a way of dying, of turning into cliché, and we have to be careful about asking all to assume the same code. Some freshness of expression could surely do us good.

Becoming a member is partly a process of "cracking the code." How would you like to join the Church and hear, "All in favor, please manifest it"? What would you do? Most people in this world are not aware that spirits "radiate," and very few think of a testimony as something you can "get." Oh, and by the way, *brothern* isn't actually a word. I know. My computer just put a squiggly red line under it.

Maybe some of our little oddities are not required. Maybe it's not absolutely necessary that we hold babies in the air, like show-and-tell, after they're blessed. But I'll have to admit, I love that stuff. I would miss those idiosyncrasies if they ever passed away. But do you understand what I'm saying? Our mannerisms are not our religion. We need to allow room for those who don't fit all the patterns.

This sort of thing takes on a really serious dimension when new members end up leaving the Church because their deacon-aged son doesn't have the "right" clothes for passing the sacrament. Or maybe the same family looks around and says, "We're not like these people. We can't afford piano lessons for our kids. We don't drive a minivan. Besides, half the time, we don't even know what they're talking about."

Can there be anything further from the spirit of what Christ taught than a culture that doesn't make new followers feel not only welcome but appreciated for their diversity?

Every group possesses a culture, and I love being a "Mormon" in the cultural sense. I love that circle of priesthood we make when we bless a child or ordain a twelve-year-old boy. I love the "brothern" in my high priest group, both for the profound things they say in a discussion and the banter of men who cheer for different sports teams. I love watching a dad carry his crying baby out of the chapel during sacrament meeting, or seeing a father bring his toddler to priesthood meeting while his wife teaches Primary. And I love Primary—all the songs and the little visual aids the choristers use. I love spotting a friend from my ward at the grocery store and feeling an instant connection. I love watching a couple in the pew in front of me in sacrament meeting, trying to keep a lid on their kids' energy for an hour and ten minutes. I love Sunday School, and teaching Gospel Doctrine, the comments people make, the old-fashioned and clichéd ones right along with the fresh and new.

It's a good life. I love the whole thing, from fire-sides to ward dinners, from fast Sunday to end-of-the-month home teaching. It's who we are, who I am.

But it's not exactly the gospel of Jesus Christ.

Elder Dallin H. Oaks, as I mentioned before, taught us the importance of "becoming," not just doing. In that same talk, he said:

> We are challenged to move through a process of conversion toward that status and condition called eternal life. This is achieved not just by doing what is right, but by doing it for the right reason—for the pure love of Christ. The Apostle Paul illustrated this in his famous teaching about the importance of charity (see 1 Cor. 13). The reason charity never fails and the reason charity is greater than even the most significant acts of goodness he cited is that charity, "the pure love of Christ" (Moro. 7:47), is not an *act* but a *condition* or state of being. Charity is attained through a succession of acts that result in a conversion. Charity is something one becomes. Thus, as Moroni declared, "except men shall *have* charity they cannot inherit" the place prepared for them in the mansions of the Father (Ether 12:34; emphasis added). ["The Challenge to Become," *Ensign*, November 2000, 34]

The gospel should run deep in us. It should be the power that says to us, "My brother is hurting; I want to relieve his pain." And it shouldn't matter whether the two of us have much in common other than the gospel. It's the voice that speaks to us and says, "She will be healed" as we lay our hands upon her head. It's the tingling sensation that comes with felt faith, with conviction, with testimony. It's a sense that we love these people, even the ones we don't like much, and it is only together that we can move ahead. It's the instant decision not to pass along a rumor and then to think the best of the victim of the gossip. It's charity— the pure love of Christ.

I picture Christ, His arms extended, inviting all of us to Him. *All of us.* We'll never understand His gospel until we understand that: that Christ welcomes all. We must not "pretend" to be His followers. It's a sin to fake something so elemental. We're weak, and we can be petty, but the challenge is to see the big picture, to feel the spirit of what Christ taught, and then to find authenticity in our belief and action.

I hear people say that we should avoid the "very appearance of evil." I suppose. But I'd rather avoid actual evil. And above all, we need to avoid the "appearance" of righteousness as we search for *actual* righteousness.

But we also have to remember that complete phoniness is rare and perfection is, in mortality, nonexistent. While we seek authenticity, we must forgive ourselves if we are sometimes a little too conscious of what others think. It's only natural that we would want to look our best even though we know we're still works-in-progress. It's just terribly important that we not overrate others as we measure ourselves and that we not settle for outward appearances when the Spirit instructs us to live a higher law.

We usually think of competition as a head-on clash, people trying to outdo one another. The competition to *appear* as good or better than others is a much more subtle contest, but it may be the most dangerous of all. We can live out our lives, going through the motions, and never notice that we missed the path we thought we were walking on.

So as we review our lives and try to understand ourselves—with the goal of making changes—I think we have to take a hard look at the image we present to the world.

What's the saying? "You can put lipstick on a pig, but it's still a pig." We all know that's true. But our challenge is much less obvious. We're not pigs. We're children of God. And God understands that we're mere children, trying hard to grow up. But we can be honest with ourselves—and with one another—as we journey toward a life of deeper integrity. I want to talk more in coming chapters about specific techniques, but I think the starting place is understanding ourselves well enough to recognize that a gap between appearance and truth exists for all of us.

We don't need to use guilt as our motivation. The point is to recognize that the desire to appear better than we are is part of the atmosphere of competitiveness that at times makes us feel the need to simulate religion, rather than live it. But the gap is there for every one of us, and God loves us all the same.

Still, it's our whole heart we want to give Him, and we can only do that when we look inside ourselves and see with His vision.

CHAPTER 6

Christ's Way

I'VE ALREADY ALLUDED TO THE questions Alma asked his people: "Have ye spiritually been born of God? Have ye received his image in your countenances? Have ye experienced this mighty change of heart?" (Alma 5:14).

Yes. We've experienced that mighty change.

If you converted to the Church, you know this awakening; you've accepted Christ's atonement and been baptized in His name. Those of us who grew up with the gospel and are committed members have "come to the faith" at some point, and we can often trace our conversion back to specific spiritual experiences.

But then in verse 26, Alma asks: "If ye have experienced a change of heart, and if ye have felt to sing the song of redeeming love, I would ask, can ye feel so now?"

Alma clearly recognized that after the mighty change comes, it can wane. My experience is that the change doesn't last forever. It's something that must be reexperienced, rejuvenated, renewed. We don't feel a steady flow of spiritual intensity, but rather intermittent boosts that reconfirm our initial change of heart.

So we think up "programs" to better ourselves— schedules and goals to keep us moving ahead. I wonder how many times I've heard Benjamin Franklin quoted in sacrament meeting. He proclaims in his famous *Autobiography*: "I conceived the bold and arduous project of arriving at moral perfection. I wished to live without committing any fault at any time; I would conquer all that either natural inclination, custom, or company might lead me into" (*The Autobiography and Other Writings on Politics, Economics, Virtue*, ed. Alan Houston [Cambridge University Press, 2006], 68).

He sounds like us!

And he thought up a sure-fire plan. He listed thirteen virtues he wanted to develop, created a chart to mark the mistakes he made, and then he stressed one virtue a week so that he could devote full concentration on it before he moved on to the next one.

Great idea!

But it didn't work.

Well, he did say he met with *some* success. He felt that he improved a little.

That's not bad, I guess. But he set out to be perfect, and what he admitted was that he fell far short, and you can guess why: "While my attention was taken up and care employed in guarding against one fault, I was often surprized [sic] by another. Habit took the advantage of inattention. Inclination was sometimes too strong for reason."

Franklin never did find the discipline to bring complete "order" into his life even though that was one of the virtues he sought. He also admitted that he made little headway with pride, the "natural passion" he found most difficult to subdue: "Disguise it, struggle with it, bat it down, stifle it, mortify it as much as one pleases, it is still alive and will every now and then peep out and show itself."

We know all about that, don't we? He was playing spiritual Whac-A-Mole, with weaknesses popping up around him and only one mallet to use against them. Still, he was right to try, and by thinking about virtues, making a list of them, and keeping them in his head, he at least had his heart in the right place. The drawback was that in making his list and checking it constantly, his daily failures were brought to his attention. And that became discouraging. He actually didn't stick with his pursuit very long.

For Latter-day Saints, the challenge is even greater. Ben Franklin only named thirteen traits he wanted to work on. We can think of hundreds. Every time we go to church we hear about things we don't do right or things we ought to be doing that we're not.

But we're not talking about competition now; we're

talking about self-improvement. At least in theory. The problem is, as I've already discussed, we tend to compare ourselves to others as we work on ourselves, and we sometimes feel pressured to make changes that have more to do with culture than with the gospel. For that reason, I want to focus in this chapter on the basics: on the behaviors and traits that Christ taught His followers.

My fear is that just as the Pharisees developed a very long list of things to do but failed to remember the spirit of the law, we're in danger of doing the same. It's easy to get so involved in the minutia of legalistic "thou shalt nots" that we forget the higher laws He introduced, or more accurately, *restored* to the world.

If we hope to become true disciples, we have to acquire a profound sense of what Christ was speaking of when He invited us to follow Him: His higher law.

I think the best statement of what Christ taught is in his greatest sermon—The Sermon on the Mount. We have Matthew's version, Joseph Smith's translation, the Book of Mormon version, and a similar sermon in Luke (perhaps another version of The Sermon on the Mount) that is sometimes called The Sermon on the Plain. Some scholars believe that He gave the same sermon, or elements of it, many times. It was the core of His doctrine.

Christ spoke to His disciples, as "multitudes" of less committed people also listened. Some have said that

He was only teaching His leaders how to live and didn't expect everyone to take on such a high standard. Certainly some sections of the sermon are expressly intended for His newly called apostles, but it's also clear that He was teaching them what they should teach others. That makes His admonitions guidance for all—both then and now. The sermon certainly asks more of us than we can possibly achieve in mortality; still, it describes the images of perfection we should keep before us.

Benjamin Franklin named twelve virtues, and then, on the advice of a friend, added "humility" to his list. With his "self-made man" approach to perfection, that isn't surprising. But Christ *started* with humility. It was the first trait he emphasized. The sermon, as we all know, begins with the Beatitudes. "Blessed are the poor in spirit," He taught, "for theirs is the kingdom of heaven" (Matthew 5:3).

In his article, "A Reading of the Sermon on the Mount: A Restoration Perspective," Brigham Young University scholar Andrew C. Skinner has explained the possible meaning of "poor in spirit":

> Presumably, it means those who are "poor in pride," those who are devoid of pride, or those who are "poor in the spirit of the world." The Greek term for "poor" used here by Matthew, *ptochoi*, originally denoted "begging," but in this passage the term

means "dependent on others for support" or even "those who are poor in the world's estimation" (Arndt and Gingrich, *A Greek-English Lexicon of the New Testament and Other Early Christian Literature,* University of Chicago Press, 2000, 728).

This fits perfectly with the fuller accounts of this beatitude in 3 Nephi and in the Joseph Smith Translation, wherein the poor in spirit are blessed or happy if they come unto Christ (3 Nephi 12:3; JST Matthew 5:5), on whom all of us are dependent. In fact, all of the Beatitudes may be read more profitably by inserting the phrase "who come unto me," for, in truth, that is the implication of all of them. We are dependent on Jesus for exaltation and lasting happiness. [Richard Neitzel Holzapfel and Thomas A. Wayment, eds., *The Life and Teachings of Jesus Christ,* (Salt Lake City: Deseret Book Co., 2005), 339–40]

In Sunday School we sometimes work our way through the Beatitudes and try to define the various types of people Christ mentions as deserving to be blessed: "the poor in spirit," "they that mourn," "the meek," "they which hunger and thirst after righteousness," "the merciful," "the pure in heart," "the peacemakers," and "those persecuted for righteousness' sake." Trying to define each one makes for an interesting discussion, but I'd rather focus on what unites all these descriptions. The basis of all of them is that most fundamental of virtues, humility.

A concise statement of the concept behind the Beatitudes might be: "Blessed are they that, through life's trials, have humbled themselves and come to Christ, and in that act, have become purified."

Franklin tried to build a perfect person from the ground up, one brick at a time. Christ starts with a principle: the mortar that holds the bricks together. He set before us the attitude—the way of life—that makes the grand concept possible. Franklin's was a rational process; Christ's was spiritual.

In effect, Christ teaches us: "If you want to be blessed (exalted), start by humbling yourself." Maybe He's even saying, "I know that you won't get everything exactly right in this life, but if you give your will over to me, you'll be all right. I'll take care of you."

And that sounds possible to me—a reasonable expectation.

Everything about living the gospel seems to be grounded in humility. Obedience is crucial, but it derives from a willingness to listen and accept. Charity manifests itself as love and acceptance of others, but that state of mind can only be achieved through humility. All the positive traits we're trying to develop come to us naturally when we feel the workings of the Spirit, and the Spirit comes to us when we're humble. It may seem as though Christ is saying, "I love those who have been kicked around." But there's more to it than that. When some people get battered, they get angry, bitter, and prideful. Christ loves those who do the opposite: the ones who trust in God and give their hearts to Him. They are the ones who open themselves to the Spirit, to obedience, to His love.

When Christ uses the word *meekness*, most of us hear that as a synonym for humility, and I believe it is. But there's a little more to it than that. We know that those with priesthood authority should act "only by persuasion, by long-suffering, by gentleness and meekness, and by love unfeigned" (D&C 121:41). In Matthew, Christ teaches that while Gentile leaders exercise dominion over others, those who would be great among His followers should minister to their people and *be their servants* (see Matthew 20:25–28).

Remember, this is not mere service as we think of it now. To be a servant at the time of Christ was comparable to being a slave. It was to obey a master. He was asking us to lower ourselves to a position that leaves no room for the slightest pride.

How then should we picture a meek person? Someone who's afraid, nervous, without confidence? Andrew Skinner wrote in the same article:

> [Meekness] might be described as poise under pressure, patience in the face of provocation. Peter's first epistle tells us that though Jesus was reviled, He did not revile

in return (1 Peter 2: 23). Meekness is one of the clearest reflections of how closely a disciple's personality or makeup, or even reactions, mirror those of the Savior.

The reward for meekness is possession of the earth. Thus, meekness is a celestial attribute, a sanctifying attribute, and it will be found in rich abundance among those who inhabit the celestial kingdom. [p. 341]

When Christ threw the money changers out of the temple, He was bold. When He told the Pharisees they were hypocrites—and said it to their faces—He was courageous. When He stood before Pilate and refused to beg for His own release, He was brave. That would indicate to me that we don't have to hang our heads and cower before the world to be meek. But Christ never placed Himself above others, never bragged, never failed to help those in need. He had ultimate power at His command, and He chose not to use it to bring importance to Himself; instead, He placed Himself among the lowly, brother to every man and woman He met.

After Christ instructs His followers that they should be meek and humble, He tells them to let their light shine. If we try to develop the personal traits Christ taught, but do so only to improve ourselves, we're forgetting Christ's example. His mission was to share His truths with all who would listen—to offer the world a path to happiness.

If we love Christ's teachings and experience them as a gift, it's fitting that we want to pass that gift to others. The metaphor of letting our light shine is not intended as a promotional concept, and certainly not as prideful boasting. There are those who are self-conscious about their own goodness. They may be doing what they think is right, but they also make sure everyone notices. Clearly, that's not Christ's way. His way was to love, to help, to teach. He offered His gospel as a gift of love and sought no gain for Himself.

The challenge is to humble ourselves, not so much by gritting our teeth and resisting our impulse to be prideful—but more by forgetting ourselves and focusing on those whose lives we can bless.

Christ introduced a higher law, a law that had been taught in earlier dispensations, before the time of Moses. He instructed His disciples not to break the law, nor to teach others to do so, but then He revealed how He felt about the attitude of the Pharisees: "For I say unto you, That except your righteousness shall exceed the righteousness of the scribes and Pharisees, ye shall in no case enter into the kingdom of heaven" (Matthew 5:20).

This is a key to what He believed and what we have to remember. The Pharisees—the rabbinical class and their followers—had created an "oral law": a tradition of interpretations of the commandments. This was a detailed set of regulations, covering such things as the preparation of food, the proper activities for the Sabbath, marital rules, and so on. We know what Christ disliked about these regulations. The spirit of the law had been lost, and interpretations involved a strictness that tended to ignore the original intent of the commandments. What was worse, Pharisees were smug in this letter-of-the law approach and harshly judgmental of those who breached it in the smallest way.

We understand that much, and we nod as Christ denounces the mean-spirited extrapolations and the downright silliness of some of the rules. We find it hard to imagine that anyone could miss the point of the gospel so completely. But if we hope to follow Christ, we certainly have to be aware of some of those same tendencies in ourselves.

Suppose one of the Pharisees had been assigned to look after a few members of his congregation, teaching and serving them. And suppose as part of his watch-care assignment that a monthly visit were required by law. And suppose this Pharisee made his visits, often on the last day of the month, but forgot the concept, the service that he was to provide those in his charge.

I know. That sounds ridiculous. But you know those Pharisees.

I think it's difficult as a Christian not to develop some of those Pharisaical traits. But that's the great difference between Christ and the old law. He asked that we bring our hearts with us to our visits, that we rise to a higher level. And He saw that need in many aspects of our lives: "Ye have heard that it was said by them of old time, Thou shalt not kill; and whosoever shall kill shall be in danger of the judgment: But I say unto you, that whosoever is angry with his brother without a cause shall be in danger of the judgment" (Matthew 5:21–22).

That seems to suggest there are good reasons, apparently, for being mad at someone at times. He does say "without a cause." Still, I can't imagine that Christ was justifying petty resentments and egoistic displays of impatience. The idea is, I think, that righteous indignation may be justified, but we should find a way to be reconciled to those we clash with, and we should work out the problem.

Christ added to His admonition that we should agree with our adversaries "quickly" (Matthew 5:25). But why should we do that? Don't we have a right to denounce stupidity and falsehood? I suppose there are different ways to read Christ's statement, but clearly He didn't mean that we have to agree with everyone's opinions. The *spirit* of what He was talking about was that we should be able to agree to disagree with others, that we respect others' opinions, and that we not sue people over every little issue that comes up (see Matthew 5:40).

There are other principles in this higher law: "Ye have heard that it was said by them of old time, Thou shalt not commit adultery. But I say unto you, That whosoever looketh on a woman to lust after her hath committed adultery with her already in his heart" (Matthew 5:27–28).

I would like to think that a thought passing through a person's mind is not tantamount to lusting to the point of mental adultery. But the Internet has brought lust into our homes at a level beyond anything we ever imagined. And now we can understand what Christ was talking about. When a person ogles prurient images and disconnects sex from love, corruption seeps into his inner self. He commits premeditated lust. I look at it this way: If we look across the street at a bank and say to ourselves, "If I thought I could get away with it, I'd walk in there and rob that place," then we've committed robbery in our hearts. The same goes with adultery.

But that's the negative side of the higher law. When any person reduces another to a sex object, thinking to get from that person something for himself, that is not only selfish, but it's destructive to the object of that intention. Love-making is more than sex-making, and our world has gone crazy with images of arousal that are divorced from love and marriage. I remember the

1960s, when women asked not to be objectified by men, but now, turnabout has apparently become fair play, because men are turned into sex objects in advertising and in movies and television. It's as though our society has reverted to some sort of adolescent preoccupation with everything sexual.

Christ asked His followers always to look higher, see a fuller context, understand the motivation behind their actions. He taught them: "Ye have heard that it hath been said, An eye for an eye, and a tooth for a tooth: But I say unto you, That ye resist not evil: but whosoever shall smite thee on thy right cheek, turn to him the other also." He then added that if any man "will sue thee at the law, and take away thy coat, let him have thy cloke also." If a man "compels" you to go a mile, go two (see Matthew 5:38–41). Joseph Smith translated this to say that if a man asks you to go a mile, go that mile—but the concept is much the same (see JST Matthew 5:43). Be meek, not combative, in dealing with others—that's the spirit of the law.

And then Christ asked the ultimate: "Ye have heard that it hath been said, Thou shalt love thy neighbour, and hate thine enemy. But I say unto you, Love your enemies, bless them that curse you, do good to them that hate you, and pray for them which despitefully use you, and persecute you; That ye may be the children of your Father which is in heaven: for he maketh his sun to rise on the evil and on the good, and sendeth rain on the just and on the unjust. For if ye love them which love you, what reward have ye? do not even the publicans the same? And if ye salute your brethren only, what do ye more than others? do not even the publicans so? Be ye therefore perfect, even as your Father which is in heaven is perfect" (Matthew 5: 43–48).

What a load to carry on our imperfect backs.

We are always quick to qualify this commandment. We've heard somewhere that the word translated as "perfect" actually means "whole" or "complete." Maybe that gives us some wiggle room. But I'm afraid we invoke this qualification and then, in effect, say, "I can't love my enemies. No mere mortal can do that."

So we decide to work on that one later.

Let's look back, though, at the whole context of this commandment. Christ was talking about a particular perfection, not offering a mere generality. He was talking about a refusal to retaliate, a desire to serve others and get along with them. He was talking about offering love for hatred, cooperation instead of belligerence. So rather than think of every possible perfection we might seek, it's more helpful to think whether we can respond perfectly—with love—when someone mistreats us.

Our "enemies," as we normally use the term, are the people we battle in a war. We don't know them. One of the reasons military training involves the dehumanizing of the enemy is so that the people on the other side don't start to seem too much "like us." But Christ didn't use war as an example. The enemies He talks about are people who hate us, treat us with spite, or persecute us.

A few years ago I had an enemy—or so it seemed. Interesting to me was how many of my fellow Saints encouraged me to be angry with him. It was almost as though those who loved me thought they had to show that love by taking my side against him and then justifying my right to hate him. That wasn't helpful. I didn't want to hate the man. Once again, people seemed to be saying, "I know Christ told us to love our enemies, but surely we can't be expected to do that."

In the abstract it may seem impossible to love one's enemy, but when we humanize our adversaries, think of them as people like ourselves—weak vessels—we *can* let our anger go.

Having an enemy is always, to some degree, our choice to define another human as an opponent. People we don't know and who oppose us take on the dimensions of villains in a melodrama. They're pure evil in our minds. But the better we know people, the harder it is to define them. The better we understand their points of view, the harder it is to see our own view as the only possible interpretation of events. The way to love our enemies is to make them human, and then to compare them not to abstract perfection but to our own humanness. Suddenly we aren't looking down on them from the heights, but across the way, from our own lowly state.

But what if someone strikes us? Can we turn another cheek? Does Christ really expect that?

Most of the blows we receive are verbal, aren't they? It's surprising what happens when we weather an insult and don't respond with our own. Few people continue their assault.

There are plenty of people around who tease in ways that are cruel, or people who throw out indirect insults in sugary voices. Even spouses play little games of that sort—criticizing a mate in front of others, for instance. Can we refuse to enter into that game? Can we say what we feel openly, perhaps even admit that those jibes do sting? Can't we hold back our own verbal volleys and even grant that in most cases people don't mean to hurt with such banter?

What Christ talked about next is something I brought up earlier. He told His disciples—and us—not to seek praise and attention when we simply do what we're supposed to do. It's good to give alms, but not if it's mainly to make ourselves look good to others. I don't know that many of us bring our prayers to the attention of others, the way Christ accused the Pharisees of doing, but certainly we like to "have our reward" by letting people know that we've complied in some way with what is expected of us. It's a natural thing for all of us to want to be thought well of, so it's hard to resist the chance to brag a little, especially if we can find a way to mention our accomplishments without sounding arrogant.

Think about the underlying principle Christ was teaching. When we demand attention for doing what's right, we would exalt ourselves, place ourselves above others. It's counter to His way.

Do we get the point about the Lord's Prayer? We often try to parse the sentences, to comprehend why this is such a good example of how to pray. But Christ's point was to demonstrate how simple a prayer could be. He had been talking about not showing off with our prayers, not using "vain repetitions," and then He gave His prayer, which was to the point, only asking for "daily bread," not lavish gifts.

I think an eloquent prayer can inspire a congregation, but I get nervous when our language gets too fancy and when the prayer goes on and on. Christ was saying that it's hypocritical to take something as righteous as prayer and turn it into a performance, a way to make ourselves look good.

And then Christ voiced the powerful admonition I started with in this book: "Lay not up for yourselves treasures upon earth, where moth and rust doth corrupt, and where thieves break through and steal: But lay up for yourselves treasures in heaven, . . . For where your treasure is, there will your heart be also" (Matthew 6:19–21).

He added, a few verses later: "Ye cannot serve God and mammon" (Matthew 6:24). And what is mammon? Our LDS Bible Dictionary says it's an Aramaic word (the language spoken in Christ's time) meaning "riches" (p. 728). You can't serve God and riches. And what would it mean to *serve* riches? Have you ever heard of debt service? Well, that's playing with words, but that's the idea. Our pursuit of riches can become obsessive and lead to our possessions owning us rather than the other way around.

So what does Christ advise on this matter? He says, "Take no thought for your life, what ye shall eat, or what ye shall drink; nor yet for your body, what ye shall put on. Is not the life more than meat, and the body than raiment?" (Matthew 6:25).

But this sounds impractical and foreign to us. Could it be one of those "as far as it is translated correctly" places in the Bible? Haven't our modern prophets told us to get a good education so that we can provide for our families? That doesn't sound like "Take no thought" about our lives. People do have to eat, and they do have to have clothing. We spend much of our lives either preparing for our vocation or actually earning a living. How can we "take no thought" of such things?

It's true, in this section, Christ probably had His

apostles in mind—leaders who would be traveling and teaching and would depend on believers for their sustenance. As missionaries, they need not think about the commonplace demands of life. They should focus entirely on their missions. And yet, there is a principle here that does apply to all of us who profess to be Christians.

I don't think He meant that we shouldn't learn how to fish if we want to be fishermen. He wasn't telling us that we don't have to bother with practical matters. In Matthew 6:32, after talking about lilies as an example for us—lilies that "toil not"—He says, "for your heavenly Father knoweth that ye have need of all these things." The Lord knows what a lily needs—sun and water—and He provides them. In the same way, the Lord knows our needs and will make sure we have them if . . . look at verse 33: "But seek ye first the kingdom of God, and his righteousness; and all these things shall be added unto you."

So it's a matter of priorities. We certainly have to concern ourselves with the everyday process of making a living, but we also have to remember what matters more. It's here that I become rather shamefaced at my petty, materialistic desires.

Christ spoke next of resisting the temptation to judge others. I've heard long dissertations on the meaning of "judge" in this passage. But let's keep the concept as simple as Christ does. Don't find fault in others, He's saying. After all, you have your own faults.

We agree immediately. But do we understand the full import of what He means? I've been saying throughout this book that we shouldn't think of life as a competition, and this scripture gets at the problem. If we think of ourselves as competing with others, we're tempted to find pleasure as we look around and see people who aren't doing as well, or any better, than we are.

Wouldn't you like to think that God watches what you do, sees your imperfections, but still thinks the best of you? Certainly He understands your circumstances, the "baggage" you carry through life, and He judges with that in mind. How can we do less for others?

And by the way, this concept goes back to loving not only our friends but our adversaries. We can't do it unless we stop making a case against them.

There's much more in this great sermon, but let's end with the rule that holds all these concepts together: "Therefore all things whatsoever ye would that men should do to you, do ye even so to them: for this is the law and the prophets" (Matthew 7:12).

It's what we call the Golden Rule: treat people the way you would like to be treated. There is no statement more basic to Christ's doctrine. Ben Franklin looked at himself and asked how he could make something better. Christ asks us to look outside ourselves, care about others, and let His Spirit rest upon us and change who we are.

So have we experienced this mighty change of heart? It's a start to feel the influence of the Spirit, but the change is not complete until we take what the Spirit tells us and enter into the life of Christ's higher law. We are not here to compete with others; we are here to forget ourselves and love our brothers and sisters.

What was Christ's *new* commandment? That we love one another. It really is as simple as that.

But there's a danger in our review of The Sermon on the Mount. I think we have a tendency to look at it as an impossible dream. We think about "doing" our home teaching, paying our tithes and offerings, not drinking alcohol, and it all sounds like stuff we can do. But love your neighbor *as yourself?* Can anyone *really* do that? Love your *enemy?* Give some guy your coat just because he asked for it? Are we supposed to take that kind of doctrine seriously?

The answer, of course, is yes. But it's revolutionary doctrine. It goes against everything "the world" teaches us. It denies the instincts of the "natural man." It really does take a mighty and lingering change in our hearts to embrace and live the concepts.

That sounds daunting. And yet, in some ways it's an easier path than the one we tend to follow. Being divided, pulled back and forth by contradictory forces, makes for a stressful, disappointing existence. Feeling at odds with others is clearly more difficult than feeling supported by and supportive of an entire community. Christ proclaimed: "For my yoke is easy, and my burden is light" (Matthew 11:30). But I think we often feel just the opposite, that we're carrying a heavy load. Is it because we're trying to pull our burden by ourselves, when in fact, He is yoked with us, willing to help?

Still, I don't think we change in an instant. First, we have to see Christ's path clearly, and that's mostly what I've been talking about so far. We have to shed a lot of nonsense we learn along the way so that we *can* see, and then we have to keep shedding that cloud of confusion that constantly drifts back in on us. And once we have the vision, we do have to receive help. Nephi taught his people, "If ye will enter in by the way, and receive the Holy Ghost, it will show unto you all things what ye should do" (2 Nephi 32:5).

It's a matter of mind and spirit: understanding what Christ asks of us, and then feeling the power through the Holy Spirit, to go forward. That's what I want to talk about in the final two chapters: some steps we can take in changing our minds, and then, in changing our hearts.

CHAPTER 7

A Change of Mind

THROUGHOUT THIS BOOK I've invited you, and me, to think about our lives, our values, our attitudes toward others and to consider how we've become who we are. I've tried to make my case that if we perceive life to be a contest, we have little chance of comprehending Christ's teachings. And if His teachings are not clear to us, we really have no hope of following in His path.

I've suggested several ways that we tend to become confused about life's purpose. We often spend our lives accumulating: chasing after possessions, status, acceptance, and recognition. We're often perplexed by how unsatisfying that chase is, even when we experience our share of accomplishments. Often we don't recognize what's wrong because we've bought into false value systems without even knowing it. Our speech is full of metaphors from war, sports, and other contests, which reinforce the notion that life is a kind of playing field, that it's all about winning and losing, and that we have to "run up the score" on the very people whom the gospel teaches us are our brothers and sisters.

Let's assume that you're with me so far, that we agree that we're here on earth to learn from Christ, to follow Him, and to move toward being like Him. Other work, other goals, have their place, and may even provide valuable experience, but they are secondary to our main purpose, and sometimes downright contrary to what we're supposed to achieve.

One of my major concerns is what we teach the next generation. Is it possible that a young person, having been told, "You've got to have a dream," can sort this out and see that the short-term dream may be to play in the major leagues or invent software worth billions, but that those goals pale in importance to the *big* dream? I think young people will see that only if we stop making them feel important when they get base hits and perhaps a little embarrassed when they back down from a fight. If we're really not quite sure we think meekness is all that great—in the practical world—how can we teach it?

I think we have to decide whether we believe Christ's doctrines or we don't. If "look out for number one" is going to be our motto, at least we should admit that Christ teaches the opposite, and then recognize that we've chosen another path. But if we believe in "love thy neighbor as thyself," we have to see clearly what the implications are. We can't claim to believe those words and then go about life grabbing for all we can get, like kids racing to gather the most eggs at an Easter egg hunt. (Anybody ever notice a little irony in the Easter egg "competition" and connecting it to the resurrection of Christ?)

If we decide that in the confusion and busyness of life, we want to keep our priorities straight and work toward *becoming*—if we want the peace that comes from getting out of the game—I want to suggest some techniques that can help.

A term used by counselors who coach people to change is "self talk." We often judge our own actions and respond to ourselves in actual words. When we do, we can have a great effect on the progress we make. Negative self talk is guilt provoking and damaging. To say to ourselves, "I'm such an idiot," or "I'm worthless," doesn't change us in a positive way. But self-glorification doesn't help much, either. The most useful self talk frames issues so that we think of them in a proper light. We can sort things out in our minds, assess the values that lead to our behaviors, and reinforce our own positive choices.

I know it can sound burdensome to think of going about our lives constantly judging our own actions, but the fact is, we do it already. The goal is to use that self talk in a productive way. It's actually helpful and calming, not a worrisome preoccupation.

At the most rudimentary level, we can use the Ben Franklin approach. We can simply notice something we need to change—and do it. It's not a technique that works very well when it comes to living the higher law. Don't try: "I'm going to love my neighbor as myself, *starting tomorrow.*" That doesn't work.

Here's an example of something that does. I was driving past a high school one day and I saw a young student crossing a rather major street—actually, jaywalking. He had reached the middle of the street, where there was an island that separated the lanes of traffic. He was holding a drink in one hand and a paper bag in the other. While he was stopped, waiting for traffic to clear, he managed to pull a hamburger out of the bag, but he didn't have enough hands to hold everything, so he dropped the bag in the middle of the street and then ran toward the school.

Do you suspect that this young man has been taught about the evils of littering? Of course he has. He's been hearing slogans about that all his life. He's been instructed by parents, teachers—and everyone else—that it's a bad thing to drop trash wherever he happens to be.

But he needed both hands, and he made a choice.

As I watched that young man that day, it crossed my mind that there are certain decisions we should make, get them into our heads, and then just never make an exception. If he had truly adopted the principle, he would have delayed the first bite of his hamburger a few seconds, finished crossing the street, and dumped the bag in a garbage can by the school. He decided to litter because 1) he wasn't thoroughly committed to the principle of not littering, and 2) it was more convenient for *him*.

Okay, he's a teenager. But I decided that day I would never be guilty of littering again. That was my self talk: "I'm not going to litter. Not at all. Ever."

You have to understand, littering was not something I had a problem with. But I wanted my decision to be clear and irrevocable.

I know that doesn't sound like a big deal, but it's had more of an effect than you might imagine. If I toss something toward a garbage can and miss, I go back and get it, and then I make sure I don't miss the second time. And every time I do that, I remind myself, "I don't litter. Ever. I've made that decision."

Telling myself that has changed how I think about myself, and it's helped me go to the next step. I often pick up trash I see along the street or on men's room floors. I know there are lots of litterbugs in this world, and I can't get to all the trash. Still, every time I pick something up and carry it to the nearest trash receptacle, I feel that I'm part of the solution, not part of the problem. I know that we can look at all the litter by the highways and decide the job is too big, and do nothing . . . or we can pick up what we can, and know we're acting positively. In the same way, we can describe ourselves as hopeless—because there are so many things we still don't do the way we should—and we can give up. Or we can make simple changes where needed and feel grateful that we've made a little progress.

What we say to ourselves about ourselves does make a difference. But we have to believe what we say. Remember the boy I talked about back in the first chapter—the one trying to throw strikes when everyone around him was shouting that he couldn't? He might have been telling himself that he *could* throw strikes, but he was hearing the other voices louder than his own. If he could have gotten a pitch over the plate at that point, he would have trusted himself a little more, and that might have started a change in his thinking. That's why it's so important that we put our thoughts into words, not go back on our commitments, and then build from there. It takes some independence, some self-reliance, to take control of things in life that we *can* control. It's important to stop letting inertia tell us what to do. Every time I set my recycling bin out in front of my house and know that there's actually very little trash from our house headed to the local landfill, I know I'm taking my attitude about littering to the next higher level.

I know what you're thinking. If only all our choices were so simple and straightforward. Most of our weaknesses are much more subtle and even seem intrinsic to our personalities. One of my problems, as I've mentioned, is that I'm often impatient and judgmental. I give people's actions the worst possible interpretation, and I judge people too harshly. I've made a decision not to be that way, but I have to work at it. Even though I often fail, I do believe that my conscious use of self talk is starting to make a difference.

One Saturday morning I needed to wash my car and didn't have much time. I decided to go to an automatic car wash where I could get the job done in about five minutes. As I drove toward the car wash and saw an empty stall, I was relieved, but to my disappointment, I saw a pickup truck turn in just ahead of me. I knew that the time it would take to get my car washed had just doubled. And then I watched that time stretch even more. The fellow in the pickup ahead of me seemed slow, apparently groping for his wallet and then digging out some bills. Finally, he inserted a couple of dollars into the slot, and things seemed to be moving along. But the machine rejected the third dollar.

I took a big breath and told myself to calm down. He started working at the bill, trying to straighten it out. He tried it again, got it rejected again, and worked at it some more.

Are you thinking what I was thinking? Those machines have a slot for a credit card. He didn't have to go through all this. But he kept at it, and I wondered how long before he realized he didn't have enough acceptable dollars and didn't know how to get the ones back that had stayed in the machine.

I was losing it. I didn't have time to sit there all morning while he fumbled with his dollar bills.

And then something occurred to me. I was acting like my old self and I had promised to be more patient.

Ta da! Self talk to the rescue.

First, I told myself that I wasn't in *that* much hurry. After all, it was a pretty day; I could chill out a little and enjoy the morning air. That changed my mood immediately.

Then the obvious hit me. I had some dollars in my wallet. I could find out whether any of mine would work for him, and then I could use my credit card when my turn came. I reached for my wallet with one hand and the door handle with the other, ready to walk up and offer my dollars for his.

Just then the "drive ahead" light came on. He'd found enough smooth dollars, or straightened his crinkled ones enough, that he'd paid for the wash.

But I was changed. I'd thought of the right thing to do—thought of *him*, not just me—and my impatience had disappeared. I pulled up to the spot by the machine, paid, and then watched the washers work their way back and forth. Once the pickup pulled out, I drove my car into the stall—and I still felt good.

This may sound like a silly decision to brag about, but I knew it was important for me. I felt better all morning. I went about my other errands reminded of my little accomplishment.

Or was it a big accomplishment? I'd thought the way Christ might have thought about the circumstances. I know that some people would have thought of it much sooner, but this patience thing is a tough one for me, and I had "overcome the world" for a few seconds and actually placed myself in that man's plight.

Every time I manage to do something like that, I know I've made a little headway. It carries over. I'm more likely to think of the same thing the next time a similar circumstance comes up. And supposing I'd thought of it sooner and had made it to the man while he was still dealing with his own frustration? Supposing I'd said, "Here, trade me dollars and see if this one will work"? (And said it with a friendly tone, so he wouldn't think I was upset about my delay.) How would that have influenced his mood? Instead of his having to worry about the guy in the rearview mirror, maybe both of us would have felt better all day.

Think through another circumstance with me. Let's say you've gone to your high school class reunion and you've run into an old friend. You always suspected yourself of being just a little sharper than this friend, but now she's president of her own company, worth millions; or he's a congressman from the great state of

. . . whatever. Maybe it's some achievement that you've dreamed of yourself. Maybe you wanted to be a weather person on the news, and that's what he or she is doing. So what do you say to yourself when you get home? What words run through your head?

Have you done this to yourself? I think most of us have given way to envy at such moments, and we either take it out on the friend (How could that guy, with no more brains than me, get where is?), or we take it out on ourselves (What's wrong with me that I didn't "go places" the way she did?).

We may believe that life is not a contest, but suddenly, there it is in front of us. My friend won and I lost.

It's at a time like this that we choose how we're going to feel—spiteful and jealous or happy for our friend. And that choice will happen, to a large degree, according to the things we tell ourselves.

You might want to stop right here and think of some positive things you might tell yourself at such a moment.

I hope you did stop, and maybe you thought of some of the things I try to say to myself when I get into this game of comparing myself to others. It helps me to think of those hummingbirds I talked about earlier: those two birds fighting over eight spigots. I ask myself: "Does someone else's joy take joy away from me? Isn't there plenty for both of us?"

Certain general conference talks have stayed with me forever, and I can call them back to mind when I need to make a decision or talk to myself about an attitude I'm taking. I quoted earlier from Elder Jeffrey R. Holland's powerful sermon, "The Other Prodigal." The ideas in that talk have come back to me many times. I've learned to call them up when I feel the pangs of jealousy. Here's another quote from that talk:

> I think one of the reasons [we become envious] is that every day we see allurements of one kind or another that tell us what we have is not enough. Someone or something is forever telling us we need to be more handsome, or more wealthy, more applauded or more admired than we see ourselves as being. We are told we haven't collected enough possessions or gone to enough fun places. We are bombarded with the message that on the world's scale of things we have been weighed in the balance and found wanting.

Elder Holland concludes:

> Brothers and sisters, I testify that no one of us is less treasured or cherished of God than another. I testify that He loves each of us—insecurities, anxieties, self-image, and all. He doesn't measure our talents or our

looks; He doesn't measure our professions or our possessions. He cheers on *every* runner, calling out that the race is against sin, not against each other. I know that if we will be faithful, there is a perfectly tailored robe of righteousness ready and waiting for *everyone*, "robes . . . made . . . white in the blood of the Lamb."

The world tells us what matters, and all too often we listen, and in doing so we fail to hear the Lord, through the Spirit, offering us a better perspective. We need to tell ourselves over and over, say it in our prayers, teach it in our lessons, discuss it in our family home evenings—the Lord loves us, doesn't favor any one of His children over another, and isn't conducting a contest. We're the ones who invented competition with one another, and if we're thinking right, we'll get out of the game. ["The Other Prodigal," *Ensign*, May, 2002, 64]

Remember how you feel after attending or listening to general conference? You hear words of that kind and you get your head straight. You feel as though you're ready to be your better self. But the words slip away. That's why it makes sense to read the talk again, later.

An effective method is to imagine the situations

that test us and think them through ahead of time. For me, I'm ashamed to admit, my jealous response kicks in when I read about a writer who is more successful than I am. But I know I struggle with that, and I'm ready. I tell myself, "Remember what Elder Holland said," and his words come back to me. The specific phrase I like to focus on is one I've used in this book: "Get out of the game." Those words trigger a clearly developed argument against my petty behavior. And it works. I'm finding more and more times when specific words from our leaders, from the scriptures, from my own thinking, are ready and waiting when I forget that larger picture we need to hold before us.

Jealousy is often visceral, almost automatic, and it comes on us without logic. Just as a hummingbird reacts by nature to compete for its sustenance, we seem to defend our egos with equal ferocity. That's why it takes some serious self talk, deeply believed, to change that way of thinking. Most of us, if given the chance, would not actually trade our lives for someone else's, even though our emotion, on impulse, tells us that we would. And so we have to say that to ourselves. We have to remind ourselves what is rich and good about our own lives. It's a time, no matter how corny it sounds, to count our blessings.

It's also time to step back and take a larger view of things, the way I've been asking us to do throughout this book. As Latter-day Saints, we're actually pretty amazing in our capacity to see hardships and "tests" as blessings. I've often said, that to a Mormon, everything is either a blessing or a blessing in disguise. That may sound almost stupidly innocent, but isn't it actually what we believe? If life is intended to provide us experiences and to help us grow, challenges are part of the "blessing" of our mortal experience. In many cases, those who have suffered most have *become* the best among us. Isn't it conceivable that in the next life there will be those who will wish they hadn't been "tested" so much by wealth and fame?

You know this stuff. We say it to each other in testimony meeting and in our discussions at church. The trick is to say it to ourselves at crucial moments, to remember it when we need it.

I recognize that our emotions rise and fall. We handle things well sometimes, and we give way to our worst impulses at other times. Certainly, people experiencing clinical depression find it almost impossible to think well of themselves. Medical help and counseling may be the only way to reverse the negative cycle of self talk in those cases, and it may take time. But it's a method that helps if we're willing to put it to work. Even those caught in the trap of addictions can go a long way toward breaking their patterns by taking positive steps and then reinforcing those actions with positive self talk.

A related way to grow and make changes in

ourselves is to look around us, see what others do, and emulate those examples rather than to react with jealousy. We recognize kindness when we see it, and we can choose to model on the best behaviors we observe. When I was in junior high, my older brother was in high school. He'd had a summer job, so he was buying his own clothes for school. But he came home, to my surprise, with two sweaters he thought I'd like—purchased with his own hard-earned money. I've never forgotten how I felt about him that day, and I've sometimes tried to "go and do likewise."

In graduate school, when I was trying to get my dissertation finished, I turned a draft in to my major professor one day and came back to school the next morning to find it in my mailbox, already read and critiqued. My professor—still my friend—was about to go out of town, and he knew I hoped to get a quick response, so he stayed up all night to get it read. I've tried in my own teaching career to remember his example. It's easy to talk to ourselves about how busy we are, how much others expect of us, how tough our lives are. When we do, we can feel sorry for ourselves and react negatively to serving others. But when we make that special effort, as my professor did, we not only do something worthwhile; we feel better about ourselves, and again, one act builds upon another.

Many years ago, Kathy recognized that I sometimes get so wrapped up in my work that I don't take a break. For Father's Day one year she bought me a set of golf clubs and encouraged me to take a day off sometimes and play. That's pretty amazing, isn't it? How many couples get into arguments about who is carrying too much or too little of the load? But Kathy thought of my needs, not her own. Recognizing her love and goodwill, I've tried to be just as considerate of her needs. (I've also tried to put those golf clubs to full use.)

I know that personal progress is never just a steady march ahead. We sometimes feel as though we're taking one step forward followed by two steps back. And some of this probably sounds naively hopeful. After all, you may be thinking, who wants to walk around all day thinking and talking to oneself about being sweet and lovely? But many of these little changes gradually become automatic and we come to think of ourselves merely as good people, trying to enjoy others and treating them the way we'd like to be treated.

It's not all about correcting problems either. We can notice our best moments, identify them through self talk, and try to build on them. During the time I served as bishop I had an experience that was powerful to me even though it was just a minor event. Two little children were sitting on the front row with their parents. When the sacrament was passed to them, the boy—who was probably two or three—took a piece of bread, but before he could eat it, his sister suddenly grabbed it from him and popped it into her own mouth. The poor little boy put up a howl in response. I'm not sure that anyone else saw what had happened, but I could see how tragically he was taking the whole thing, and I felt sorry for him. I looked around to get the attention of a deacon, but they were not looking my way. The intensity of the little boy's crying wasn't dying down and suddenly, on impulse, I got up, walked to the sacrament table and got one of the extra trays of bread. I took it to the little boy.

I doubt that many in the chapel noticed what I had done, and I'm sure no one remembers, but it was life-changing for me. As I stood in front of the child and held out the tray, his crying suddenly stopped. He looked up at me with wonder in his face and enormous appreciation—and he took the bread and ate it.

Are you confused? As I said, it was just a little thing. But in all my years as bishop, I never had such a powerful moment of realization that I was doing what Christ would have done. The boy stopped crying immediately, and he looked at me with eyes full of love. When I sat down again, I realized, I wanted to feel that way always—and wouldn't—but I at least wanted to feel that way as often as I could. I've used that moment as a motivator to put myself in other situations in which I can bless a life.

I want to switch gears now. Maybe I'm making per-sonal change sound terribly difficult when it's actually not as difficult as it sounds. Remember Benjamin Franklin's words: "I conceived the bold and arduous project of arriving at moral perfection." If we think in those terms, that we've taken on the job of doing a complete makeover on ourselves, of turning a petty little creature into a God-like being, it's too big of a job; it's even arrogant to imagine that much "self help." What Christ asks us to do in this life is enter into a path that leads to perfection, but we have to realize that we can only get there in the eternities, and certainly not without great help from the Spirit. We can't beat up on ourselves every time we recognize that we're still frail and human.

Here's the other danger: We can set out to make ourselves perfect and become completely self-absorbed in the process, contradicting the very spirit of our endeavor. After a Sunday School class, when I had expressed my concern about the guilt I feel as I probe my motivations and come up wanting, a sister in my ward said to me, "I guess I just don't think that deep. I just sort of go along and do my best." Or words to that effect.

My first impulse was to think, "Well, yes, I guess I am pretty deep," until I thought of her. She's a lovely woman who cares about people and lives a wonderful life. She clearly reaches out to others without dwelling on herself as much as I do. She's probably miles ahead of me in getting where she wants to go.

Or in other words, self talk helps, and getting a bigger picture in our heads can help, but we also have to avoid the dangers of self-absorption. Maybe the higher law in this case is to get to the point where so much inner struggle isn't necessary—where we instinctively think mostly of others and that attitude almost automatically lifts us above much of the pettiness we normally struggle with.

Isn't that a principle Christ also taught us? Doesn't He ask us to forget ourselves? When I see people who carry out their Church assignments with real commitment, look after their neighbors, treat people with kindness, draw little attention to themselves, I think, surely the Lord is pleased. This is what He asks of us. We don't have to enter a competition to *seem* the most righteous or to imply our own righteousness in our talks or lessons or discussions.

At a BYU devotional, Bonnie D. Parkin, former general president of the Relief Society, quoted Sister Camilla Kimball, wife of Spencer W. Kimball. Sister Kimball advised women never to "suppress a generous thought." Sister Parkin built on that idea and explained to the students that they could find their personal ministries in this life and emulate Christ in their service. "Ministering," she said, "involves extending charity— the pure love of Christ—to others, one person at a time." And she added, "Most ministering opportunities are spontaneous, not planned in advance. Much of the

Savior's ministering seemed almost incidental, happening while He was on His way to somewhere else—while He was doing something else" (BYU Devotional, 13 February 2007).

Sister Parkin suggested that the students pray to be the answer to someone else's prayer, to ask for the chance to provide needed services to others. And she talked about the decision we all need to make:

> May I suggest that finding your personal ministry begins with making a decision about a consistent way of being: a way that seeks to nurture, to be entirely helpful—not just now and again, but always. Ultimately, it is a decision to further consecrate ourselves to the Lord, to more fully take upon ourselves His name—to do as He did. Making this decision deepens our connectedness to one another and to the Lord. Such a responsive way of being is who we really are—from before this life.

That doesn't sound so hard, does it? I know we have selfish impulses, but we also know the joy of serving. Choosing to be open to those better impulses, ready to serve when and where we can, never stifling an impulse to be kind and generous—it's a formula for a happy life. It's a matter of deciding who we are and whose we are, and it isn't complicated. Thinking of life as a contest makes each day feel like a grind, a fight, a series of disappointments. Thinking of life as an opportunity to serve is a release from all that.

President Ezra Taft Benson taught us that "Fear of men's judgment manifests itself in competition for men's approval. The proud love 'the praise of men more than the praise of God.'" (John 12:42–43). ("Beware of Pride," *Ensign,* May 1989, 5). And it really does come down to that. We can listen to the world, worry about our status, our worth, our importance, or we can feel the love of Christ and enter upon His path. We don't have to worry about beating anyone to the end of that path, getting there first. We don't have to promote ourselves to the Lord, develop a fancy résumé for Him, "dress for success," or practice our post-life interviewing skills. We can look about ourselves, see who needs our help, do our best each day, and then go before Him without shame.

The Lord has promised to help us along the way, and what source of strength could be more powerful? The road to perfection sounds hard, but putting our lives in the hands of God is easy. Remember that image of His yoke: it's easy because He's next to us, pulling with us. And no one, taking on a yoke, sets out running. It's an even pace, and a peaceful one.

I have the feeling that one thing that would help all of us would be to simplify our lives so that there's more room in our day to feel the Spirit, interact with friends and family, and respond with calmness. Much of our anger and frustration come from our over-commitment of time, which often comes from our over-commitment to do everything, have everything, and keep up with our neighbors. We turn holidays such as Christmas into such productions that we end up stressed and cranky instead of moved by our love of Christ. We buy houses bigger than we need and then spend every spare minute trying to make enough money to pay for them and furnish them. We worry so much about winning the games we play that we leave little time for the very things that would help us most: time with our families, scripture study, good music—all the things that build our spirits.

Maybe, more than any single thing that would change our lives, we should get out of the game, as Elder Holland said, take a deep breath, and let the Spirit speak to us. That Spirit might be telling us, "Look in on Sister Smith; she's so lonely since her husband died"; "Shovel Brother Johnson's walks. It's hard for him to do that now"; "Say hello to the kids in the ward. Call them by name." And a lot of other things. We long for a better world, a softer feel to life, a sense of wholeness, and maybe it's all right there for the having—and we're too busy to notice.

So which is it? Using self talk to change ourselves, or responding spontaneously to the Spirit? For me, I'm still not far enough along to respond as I should without working at it. I still have too many things about myself that I need to change, too many habits that I need to break. But my hope is, I'll come to a place where my reactions merely become part of who I am. I'm working to change my thinking, but ultimately, I want a change of heart that remains as close to permanent as possible. And that's the subject of the final chapter of this book.

CHAPTER 8

A Change of Heart

TOWARD THE END OF THE TIME that I served as bishop, Christmas fell on a Sunday. As we sang Christmas hymns in sacrament meeting, I found that tears were running down my cheeks. I was struck, as never before, with the realization of how much I loved the people in my ward.

But I'm a skeptic. When I receive a spiritual manifestation, the first thing I do is question it. The thought that came to me that day was that I was experiencing nothing more than emotion from the beautiful music and all the sensations we feel at Christmas. Still, the idea that kept pressing on my mind was, "I love these people. Every single one of them." So I tested the proposition. Our choir was singing several numbers and during that time I started on one side of the building, on the front row, and I let my eyes focus on each of my ward members one at a time—adults, children, everyone. I worked my way through the entire congregation. What I discovered was that I did feel love toward every one of them—honest, powerful love.

I knew these people. I knew their quirks, and I knew some of the baggage they carried with them through life. I knew the little mistakes they had made, the problems they sometimes had in their families, and I knew the major tests they had faced. I knew their sorrows. I also knew how hard some of them had worked to repent. Certainly some of them could be annoying at times, or prideful and even belligerent, but I often knew about their backgrounds, their life stories, so I understood some of the factors that had made them who they were.

Over my years as bishop, I had come to feel close to most of those people, but on that Christmas Sunday I experienced something more. I loved them in a pure way that went a step beyond anything I'd known previously. I think I experienced the pure, Christ-like love called charity.

While I was feeling that love, I couldn't have hurt anyone or anything. I don't think I could have sinned. The "natural man" in me seemed to vanish, and I basked in the knowledge that a mantle was upon me and that I was blessed to serve these particular people. I wanted the best for them. Nothing could have been more foreign than the idea that I was in competition with them. Maybe at other times I compared our houses, our cars, our clothes, our incomes, but not that day—at least not that hour.

I've wondered what it would be like to feel that way toward everyone all the time. I'm afraid it sounds a little too gooey to me as I think about it now, but it didn't then, not when the Spirit was teaching me, lifting me, filling me up.

During the years I knew the members of my ward so well, I was less judgmental than at any time in my life. It was partly the calling, partly the closeness a bishop experiences with the members, but it was also an altered self-expectation. I felt the responsibility to be as much like Christ as I was capable of being. For me, and I suspect for most people, charity toward others seems easy at times, and then, in other situations, that harsh voice sounds in our heads. Clearly, when moved by the Spirit in church or while sitting in the temple, we tend toward our better selves, but the challenge for all of us is to feel that way much more often.

I've written in the earlier chapters about the importance of thinking right, and that's essential, but it can only take us so far. To change ourselves—and stay changed—we need divine help. Some of the best advice we can follow, in seeking the Spirit, comes to us from King Benjamin in the Book of Mormon, who taught:

> For the natural man is an enemy to God,
> and has been from the fall of Adam, and will
> be, forever and ever, unless he yields to the

enticings of the Holy Spirit, and putteth off the natural man and becometh a saint through the atonement of Christ the Lord, and becometh as a child, submissive, meek, humble, patient, full of love, willing to submit to all things which the Lord seeth fit to inflict upon him, even as a child doth submit to his father. [Mosiah 3:19]

The more we foster the influence of the Holy Ghost in our lives, the more likely we are to feel less of that competitive, judgmental attitude. And the key to putting off our natural inclinations, our competitiveness, is to become submissive, meek, humble, patient, full of love. For King Benjamin, just as for Christ in the Sermon on the Mount, the first step is humility.

But I'm not a bishop now, and I find it harder to keep that Spirit with me. What can help me recover that outlook? The Sunday School answer for that question is, "Read the scriptures and pray." And no doubt that is a big part of the answer, but you and I have both discovered ways to run our eyes over the words in a chapter of the scriptures, "say" a quick prayer, and feel that we've done our duty—without gaining much spiritual benefit. If we are truly to get in touch with the Spirit and surrender completely to its influence, we must *study* the scriptures, *search* the scriptures. We work our way through the standard works in seminary, in institute, in Gospel Doctrine class, but many don't get around to reading their assignments, and often, the one who really studies is the teacher. That's only normal, of course; but if we are to completely throw off the natural man and finally acquire a real feel for Christ, His life, and His teachings, it's going to take more than a superficial effort.

My opportunity came when I taught Gospel Doctrine for five years. That experience helped me more than anything I've done—other than serve as bishop. Through most of my life I have served in bishoprics and busy administrative positions. I went through the motions in fits and starts of studying the scriptures, but mostly, I "read" them. Finally, while teaching the whole cycle of the four-year scripture study program, I developed a fuller knowledge of the history and context of the scriptures, and more important, my understanding of Christ and His teachings deepened.

Kathy and I were lucky enough to travel to Israel, too, and that gave us a chance to see the paths Christ walked, the towns He visited, and to more vividly picture the culmination of His work in Gethsemane and on Golgotha. Being in those settings was a life-changing experience for both of us.

What I've found lately is that I can pick up the New Testament and read a passage, and the background I gained during those teaching years comes back to me, at least in large measure. In other words, I can now get more out of my reading. I also forget things, so it's very important that I check cross references, look up concepts in the Bible Dictionary, refer to background books, etc. The more I *study*, not just read, the more influence the scriptures have on me.

Still, given the demands of living, there are periods when we can't sit and study for an hour each night. I think of young mothers or people with demanding callings in the Church. There are times when we may have to settle for simply reading the scriptures, and only reading for short periods. But reading even a few verses can make a difference in our day, especially if we are reviewing something that we've come to know well. I think, too, it's crucial to take part of that time, however short, to ponder what we've read. If we can at least read the assignments for Gospel Doctrine class, it will keep us in touch with the doctrines Christ taught. Even more, it reminds us of the model we hope to follow: His meekness, His goodness, His charity.

It goes without saying, when our prayers are offered out of routine, they don't help us much. My desire is always to pray sincerely, even when I'm not in a time of crisis. But it's hard to be consistent about that, isn't it?

One thing we know is that mortality is supposed to be difficult. We don't ask for tests, but they inevitably come. Certainly we should hope to grow spiritually in times of prosperity, and not let our good lives ruin us, but most of us, in retrospect, are also thankful for the hard times we pass through. During that time that I taught Gospel Doctrine, I also experienced a long, drawn-out period of worry and challenge. Given my spiritual outlook at that time, my reaction was to humble myself and seek help. I'm not eager for another experience of that kind, but I am thankful for the way I was able to use that time to deepen my faith.

But that raises the bigger question: How can we be humble and willing to listen to the Spirit when we are *not* compelled to do so by a special calling or a major worry? I was home teaching recently, and I asked my friends Dick and Brenda Hines what helped them keep the Spirit with them. Dick offered a really interesting approach. He, too, has served as a bishop, and he also found himself powerfully changed by his love for his ward members, the same as I did. But after his release, he wanted to hold onto the spirituality he had gained. He found that what worked for him was to say to himself, as he interacted with others, "I really love that brother," or, "What a great person; I really love her." Dick told me that saying the words seemed to set off feelings that not only helped him treat that one individual well but carried over to the way he felt and acted all day.

I think that's a wise approach, and I've been trying

it. What I find is that it works well until I get a little disgusted with someone and feel in no mood to say such a thing. But that's where Brenda's advice comes in. In response to what her husband had said, she told me that her version of the same thing was to concentrate on thinking the best of people, of interpreting their behavior in the best possible light—and doing it consciously. For her, it's a choice to put herself in the other person's shoes, and do it in specific words, so that her attitude actually changes.

There may be other similar techniques, but the key, I think, is to think the way Christ might think about His brothers and sisters. When we're doing that, we can't get too far away from the Spirit. Anger and rudeness seem impossible. The key is to find a mental trigger that causes that higher law, that big picture, to click into focus—and at the same time create the emotions that open us to the influence of the Lord.

After we'd talked about all that for a time, my home teaching partner, Wayne Mitchell, said that serving people helped him most but then admitted that it's easy to get too busy and not pay attention to others' needs. He and his wife, Cheri, are trying now, each Sunday, to identify people they might serve in some way, so that they don't just talk about what they ought to do, but make specific plans.

If you're a skeptic like me, you're probably thinking that these techniques sound good in theory, but the natural man lurks awfully close to the surface and rises up as a "natural" response. I admit, it's hard to break the habits we've formed and to let go of some of our negative reactions to people. Still, if we can find mental triggers that work for us, and make them part of us, it really can make a difference. It takes concentration to change such habits, but one thing is clear to me after working at this for a time: it's actually easier to let things go, cast off anger, hold back hurtful comments, than it is to act impulsively and then live with the resulting regret.

Sometimes, in the Church, we refer derisively to "Molly Mormons" and "sweet spirits," and maybe we resent (or are jealous of?) the insipid niceness that we sometimes see in fellow members. But think about that. Aren't we really bothered only when someone seems to be faking sweetness? Aren't we drawn to and don't we love people who are generous and kind and who clearly love us in spite of our faults? I'm not saying that we use self talk and mental triggers so we can *seem* to be better people. I'm saying that we can use these methods to become who we want to be, to keep right perspectives before our eyes, to treat people the way Christ would treat them, and in doing so, become more like Him.

If Christ dropped by for family home evening sometime, would you say afterwards, "Well, he's just a little too *nice* for my taste"?

We each have to find our own ways to keep Christ's image before us, and there are probably many ways. In the talk by Elder Jeffrey R. Holland that I quoted before, after he discussed the jealousy the good son felt toward his prodigal brother, Elder Holland described our tendency as humans to compare ourselves to one another and feel diminished by someone else's accomplishments. And then he said:

> How can we overcome such a tendency so common in almost everyone? For one thing, we can do as these two sons did and start making our way back to the Father. We should do so with as much haste and humility as we can summon. Along the way we can count our many blessings and we can applaud the accomplishments of others. Best of all, we can serve others, the finest exercise for the heart ever prescribed. But finally these will not be enough. When we are lost, we can "come to ourselves," but we may not always be able to "find ourselves," and, worlds without end, we cannot "save ourselves." Only the Father and His Only Begotten Son can do that. Salvation is in Them only. So we pray that They will help us, that They will "come out" to meet and embrace us and bring us into the feast They have prepared. ["The Other Prodigal," *Ensign*, May 2002, 64]

I see in Elder Holland's advice a process. And once again, it begins with humility. We turn—or return—to the Father by humbling ourselves. If there's one thing I've come to understand in this life, it's that humility is the core of the spiritual life. It is powerful in its powerlessness. It gives up ego and pride and it lets the Spirit in. It's the first step in repentance, but it's also, in its own way, the muscle behind every step we take on Christ's path.

Elder Holland suggests that being grateful also helps. When we recognize the goodness of our own lives, we're less likely to envy others. And when we acknowledge that all we have comes from God, we're much less likely to feel prideful. That's one reason that sincere prayer, full of thankfulness, can make such a difference in our lives.

But ultimately, Elder Holland reminds us, we have to recognize that only the Lord can lift us to that higher level of spirituality. We may not need to repent for a dissolute life, as the prodigal son did, but the principle is the same. In order to receive the influence of the Holy Ghost, we may need to "return to the Father" in our own way.

I think, for instance, of people who harbor anger toward another person. I've known people who cling to resentments and let those ugly feelings do serious damage to their own spiritual lives. It was surprising, when I was bishop, to hear from my ward members how often the animosity they were clinging to was toward a sibling or parent, or a former friend. Not quite so surprising were the ill feelings toward a former spouse. But I also saw the miracles that occurred when people let go of those hateful feelings.

"Making our way back to Father" may be different for each of us, but finally, it's a trip we have to repeat often in our lives.

For me it's fighting that skepticism I've talked about, eliminating my tendency to want all the answers. The Lord has been patient with me, and I feel loved because of it. What I notice time and time again is that when I trust the Spirit and don't battle but instead surrender to it, the power is there for me.

There's another aspect to keeping the Spirit with us that I've been thinking about lately. I've learned that certain influences are negative for my spiritual life; others are helpful. We know the obvious ones. We certainly have to be careful about the entertainment we choose. But here again, we tend to follow the pack more than we need to. I know Latter-day Saints who wouldn't watch an R-rated movie if someone held a gun to their heads. But they'll watch *anything* if it's rated PG-13. Does that sound like the Pharisaical approach to you? It does to me. I think it's important to read reviews and know what we're going to see. The ratings are created by movie makers themselves, and they often don't tell us much. There's plenty of trash that is rated PG-13.

I find that I need to fine-tune my own choices. I've talked about sports in this book because I often *care* way too much about how certain games turn out, and I've learned that a kind of intense, almost combative attitude can set in if I don't keep track of what is obvious to people who pay less attention to sports. Nothing is quite like the righteous indignation of the sports fan who *knows* that a referee has made a bad call. I've heard hatred come out of bleachers or grandstands that's foreign to everything we believe—and I've heard it at a certain university where it shouldn't exist. The trouble is, I've heard it in my own head and even coming out of my own mouth.

For that reason, for me, it has worked better to back away from sports a little. That's no recommendation to others. It's just what I've found best for my own spirit. I take the games too seriously, so I'm better off paying less attention to them and not letting them bring out the worst in me.

I find that listening to good music, by contrast, heightens my spirituality. I know that not everyone likes classical music, and so again, I'm not making a recommendation. I'm merely trying to find things that elevate *me*, soften *me*, and I'm trying to avoid the things that don't work so well. I just think that enough of us don't give thought to that. We know for sure that pornography is evil, but we don't think as much about the negative influence of inane TV sitcoms with the corrupt morals they portray and the adolescent, "nasty" humor they depend on for laughs. There are so many great books to read—from biography and history and theology to quality fiction—and all too often we let our entertainment be dictated by "the tube."

It's not that we have to feel lofty, spiritual feelings every hour of the day. I don't think it's realistic to expect that we can. There are lots of good things in life that we wouldn't call "spiritual." I love to think. I love to learn. I love to laugh. I like jazz music, and I like riding my bicycle. I like to play golf, watch track meets, go fishing, and get into marshmallow-gun fights with my grandchildren. I like to eat, and I love ice cream, and I like to watch the deer that sometimes wander past my house out back. I like to walk up Snake Creek Canyon with Kathy, and I like to have an evening when I can just sit and read. There are so many pleasures, and we often fear that the pleasures of the world are in conflict with spiritual things. Certainly, some of them are. But I love what the Lord revealed regarding the beauty and pleasure to be found in what He provided when He created this earth:

> Yea, all things which come of the earth, in the season thereof, are made for the benefit and the use of man, both to please the eye and to gladden the heart; Yea, for food and

for raiment, for taste and for smell, to strengthen the body and to enliven the soul. And it pleaseth God that he hath given all these things unto man; for unto this end were they made to be used. [Doctrine & Covenants 59:18–20]

But we each have to choose our activities wisely, enjoy the good things of the world, but make time also for the most inspiring things. The Prophet Joseph was known for enjoying life, not hiding from it, and then also drinking deep the spiritual manifestations that were granted to him.

I think it's important that we explore every means to drink in the good things, and choose those things that enrich ourselves and our families. When our kids were still twelve and under, we moved home to Utah, where Kathy and I had grown up. I had never skied, and Kathy hadn't skied since she was young. So we decided that all of us would take lessons together. I have great memories of those days, all of us on the bunny hill, trying out our new skills, then riding home together, laughing and singing Beatles songs together. But the best was the time we spent on the lifts. We would ride in combinations of two or three or four, and there was time to sit next to one another and talk. I'm afraid I may have sounded at times in this book as though I'm advocating an ascetic life in which every second is spent concentrating on fighting off our worst impulses. Far from it, I think the good life incorporates good entertainment or activities that allow us to enjoy other people, especially members of our own families.

One of the loveliest evenings of my life was spent with my family in Germany. We had just picked up our older son from his mission and then driven to my former mission in southern Germany. In the old city of Heidelberg we stayed in a hotel just around the corner from where I had lived as a young elder. That night, all staying in one room—and our first night together as a family after two years of separation—we talked about our years in Missouri when the kids were little, and in Provo when they were teenagers. We sat up late and shared dozens of stories. We felt so much love that the Spirit seemed to be filling up the air around us.

It's important that we create such experiences, that we use Christmas and other holidays, picnics, and family parties to build closeness, but also to invite the Spirit. One of the reasons we ought to simplify Christmas is so that there's enough time and calmness to talk and share and pray together. What we have to trust is that the Lord is waiting for us to call on Him. And the Spirit is waiting to fill us when we are open to its influence.

I think we all need to take a hard look at the ways we spend our time, and agree with our families on some of the things that we can discard or at least cut back. Elder Dallin H. Oaks has given us some excellent guidelines. He said that we often fill our lives with good things and fail to leave time for the better and best things (see "Good, Better, Best," *Ensign*, November 2007, 104–08). There are plenty of people in this world who fill their time with bad things, but Latter-day Saints probably have to worry more about a life of leagues and lessons, meetings and . . . general busyness.

It's a difficult problem to solve. Kathy and I are terrible examples of people who are too busy. We never cease finding things to keep us on the run. But we have begun to ask ourselves more seriously lately, what things we really need to do, and what things keep us feeling as though we're on a treadmill.

It may seem counterintuitive to suggest that we simplify our lives and then to preach that we serve in the kingdom with all our hearts, but Elder M. Russell Ballard taught us to be wise in the way we carry out our responsibilities and how to find that balance:

> I would like to let you in on a little secret. Some of you have already learned it. If you haven't, it's time you knew. No matter what your family needs are or your responsibilities in the Church, there is not such a thing as "done." There will always be more we can do. There is always another family matter that needs attention, another lesson to prepare, another interview to conduct,

another meeting to attend. We just need to be wise in protecting our health and in following the counsel that President Hinckley has given often to just do the best that we can. ["O Be Wise," *Ensign,* November 2006, 19]

We can serve well and still be careful not to overdo. Elder Ballard suggests in the same talk a way that can happen. He says that some people "start believing that the programs they administer are more important than the people they serve. They complicate their service with needless frills and embellishments that occupy too much time, cost too much money, and sap too much energy" (p. 18).

I believe that. Relief Society teachers don't have to carry flora and furniture from home to decorate the Relief Society room, and they don't have to prepare twenty-two stapled handouts. Men, who don't seem to have much trouble with those kinds of frills, may be guilty, especially as leaders, of failing to set a clear agenda. In doing so, they extend the length and frequency of organizational meetings far beyond necessary.

Clearing out a little time in our lives is crucial. If we can find an hour on a Sunday afternoon or on some evenings, get away from TV and other attractions, and spend that time with the scriptures or with the right kind of books and perhaps with good music, we can bring the Spirit into our lives.

I know what my daughter Amy would say in response: "Yeah, Dad, you and Mom are all alone; of course you can find those times. Try it with four young children." And she is *right*. It's much harder at certain times of our lives. But we do find time for things that don't build us, and taking a look at those things and cutting some of them out of our lives is certainly a start in the right direction.

Amy keeps herself so busy serving others that Kathy and I sometimes have to warn her not to take on too much. True, her service often brings the Spirit into her life, but sometimes it has led her into over commitment that results in frustration and has the opposite effect.

I'm not sure, as committed Church members, that we're ever going to have a lot of time to lie in our hammocks drinking lemonade. But we can try to find balance.

A few days ago, I was trying to get this book finished and feeling under the gun. Kathy and I had tickets to a play on a Friday, but we had had to change the tickets to Thursday because our home owners' association was meeting Friday, and we felt a need to be there. There was also a wedding reception we wanted to get to after the meeting. So on Thursday night, I drove home from Provo, a forty-minute drive, and then

Kathy and I left almost immediately for Salt Lake, a slightly longer drive. We grabbed a quick sandwich, saw the play, and then headed home. I was planning to write all day on Friday, but when I got home there was a call on my answering machine. A member of the leadership of my high priest group was looking for a crew to help someone move into our ward. I groaned. I needed as many hours as I could get. It's true that I work at home, but it's still my job. Besides, my ankle had been hurting all evening for no reason I knew of. (You've heard of old age? Well . . . I think I've got it.)

Kathy woke me up the next morning by saying, "Should we read the scriptures now? It's the only time we'll have to do it." I pried my eyes open, and we read from the book of Jacob—good stuff—and then we had our morning prayers. To get out of helping the people move, I felt like praying for severe pain in my ankle, but that was gone, also for no reason I knew of. So I called Brother Pugmire, hoping that he had found enough men. But he was still looking, and he promised we'd only be there an hour.

I almost turned him down, but then I thought, "How can I sit at home and write purple paragraphs about serving others and not serve when I'm called to do so?" So I said I'd help, and then I worked hard on this chapter, fifth or sixth draft (except for this part) until I had to go. For once, we really were there for only an hour, so I got home, showered, and got back to work. I'll admit, I played one game of Spider Solitaire just to calm myself, but I lost a close one and didn't give in to the impulse to play a second game. (Was that an act of giving up a good thing for better and best things? Probably not.)

In the meantime Kathy had gone to Salt Lake with Sister Sullivan, our Relief Society president, to get a load of ordered materials for 72-hour kits. The trouble was, we had agreed to return to Salt Lake later in the day because Kathy's father was having a special dinner at his retirement home, and Kathy felt it meant a lot to him to have us come. So for Kathy that was three trips to Salt Lake in two days, and two for me, with one to Provo thrown in (and by the way, I do feel guilty about all the emissions we were belching into the air). I also needed to run to Heber City, only ten minutes away, to get a refill on my blood pressure medicine. (I am *not* making this up. I may be a fiction writer, but this story is entirely too implausible for fiction.) So I made that run, got this chapter in better shape, and realized I would have to come back to the whole book, revise it one last time on Monday and probably Tuesday, even though I'd promised to have it in a week earlier. (Oh, and one other thing. At the drugstore my ankle started hurting again, for no reason I know of. I think that's called dramatic irony. Or maybe there was divine intervention so I was able to help with the move.)

There is a point to all this.

It was actually a nice day. I like to write, but I also enjoyed the brethren from my high priest group, and I met a new family. Kathy and I had time to talk as we drove to Salt Lake, and her father really appreciated our being with him. We knew we had done the right thing, too, to attend the home owners' meeting and the reception.

Do you hear what I'm saying? I don't think we can stop being busy. Life doesn't seem to allow it. But we were doing lots of things that needed to be done, and much of the day really was spent in looking out for others. It wasn't a rat-race day of competition and hostility; it was just a busy day full of mostly "better" things. We need to simplify, in relative terms, but I doubt life is going to be lazy for very many of us, at least in the near future. Still, if I'm serving, laughing with my brethren, chatting with my father-in-law (whom I do love), I'm happy. When life feels like a fight, my blood pressure probably rises, but carrying a heavy couch is good for me, both in terms of exercising my body and in engaging my spirit. (Even if my back still hurts today, and it *is* Tuesday, and the book still isn't finished.)

A "mighty change" may start with an intense feeling of conversion, but my experience is that keeping that gain and extending it is a lifelong project, built on daily, simple choices.

A friend of mine reminded me of a scripture that I'd

never thought much about. It's one used in *Preach My Gospel*, however, so maybe most people have considered it already. For me, it gets to the heart of what we must do to achieve that mighty change of heart.

The scripture is Moroni 8:26:

> And the remission of sins bringeth meekness, and lowliness of heart; and because of meekness and lowliness of heart cometh the visitation of the Holy Ghost, which Comforter filleth with hope and perfect love, which love endureth by diligence unto prayer, until the end shall come, when all the saints will dwell with God.

For me, this arranges the steps we have to follow into a clear, simple order. We have to repent, and that means seeing what is wrong with us, not justifying our vanities and false values. If we repent of chasing the wrong goals, recognize our pride, our lack of kindness, our harsh judgment of others, our hypocrisy, and our love of wealth, we are blessed with humility. Thus humbled, we can have the Holy Ghost with us. We all know that experience. And when we're moved upon by the Holy Ghost, we can experience, at the highest level, a perfect love—the kind of love I felt in sacrament meeting that Christmas day.

Under the influence of that kind of love, values tend to fall into place. We don't feel to compete with our brothers and sisters; we don't harshly judge, we don't care about things that don't matter. But it's hard to keep those feelings, so what do we do? Moroni says we can endure by "diligence unto prayer." And what should we pray for? I think we should repent in our prayers and pray for humility. And that starts the positive cycle over.

The mere act of thinking about these things can help. I concentrate on being a polite driver these days, and when I start to get impatient, I talk to myself. I remind myself that I want to live with a spirit of kindness, meekness, goodness. But sometimes it's an act of sheer will, because kindness is not necessarily my natural state. But on days when I have prayed for the right spirit, have studied the gospel, or for whatever reason, am feeling the spirit of the Holy Ghost with me, driving with kindness is easy. I think the goal should be to stay as close to that Spirit as we can.

I went in to pick up my car recently, after having it serviced. No one could find my paperwork or even my keys. It was one of those times when I sometimes come unglued, but I've been working on this book, thinking about all this stuff. There was an older woman waiting behind me, so I told the woman who was trying to find my paperwork to take care of her first. (I really did; I'm not making this one up.) The woman at the desk began to help the other customer, but her phone kept ringing, and people kept approaching her desk, asking questions. I finally laughed and said, "I'd go crazy if I had to do what you're doing. I'd be hyperventilating by now." She hadn't smiled until that moment, but suddenly she beamed, and she talked about the craziness. And it wasn't long until someone came in with my paperwork and keys. She thanked me for being so patient, and she gave me two car-wash certificates instead of one. I walked out feeling great, knowing that I was the person I wanted to be—at least for a few minutes. I felt meek.

I doubt that many Latter-day Saints say to themselves, "I need to work on my meekness today." But we have chances to be kind, respectful, polite—meek—every day. There are times to be indignant, to stand up for what's right, to be bold in proclaiming the truth, but if we do those things in a spirit of self-righteousness or domination, we lose what we set out to gain. At the very heart of Christ's doctrine is humility, and the world teaches us over and over not to trust in it.

In the end, Christ will make up the difference. If our treasure is right, our hearts will be right, and the Lord will love us, forgive us, and invite us back to Him. What I've had to learn is that I am important—and that I always was—but not because of anything I've done in my life. It's merely that I'm a child of God. He knows me and loves me, and I love Him. We're all exactly equal, all brothers and sisters, and we don't need to prove anything to each other. We're all weak, and we have varying talents, but we're not in a contest. Satan would love to have us believe that we're all competing for the good things of life. The truth is there's no limit to God's love. We don't have to outdo anyone to get it.

This year on the Fourth of July, six of our grand-children were with us, and through an unusual set of circumstances, two of the moms were there but not any dads. And then Kathy and my daughter and daughter-in-law ran off and left me with the kids. My grandchildren were excited about fireworks that evening and about all the other things going on, and they were rather hyped up. I was trying to keep a little control.

Kathy and I actually had spent quite a bit of time with our grandkids that summer. In fact all nine, and their parents—seventeen of us in all—had spent a week together at Aspen Grove, in the Utah Wasatch Mountains. With so many of us in one big cabin, I'm afraid I'd gotten rather grouchy with the kids at times during that week, and I still felt bad about that. One of the things I'd harped about was their running around outside without shoes, which I didn't think was safe.

Well, on that July 4, I had brought the subject up again—rather firmly—and I worried that I was being too impatient again. It's something I'd thought a lot about. My own Grandpa Pierce was an exceptionally patient, good-natured man, and I've often thought that I want to pass his legacy to my grandchildren.

All those things had been on my mind that day, but I had still gotten after them about the bare feet. And then my little six-year-old Katie came limping into the house. She was walking on one foot and one heel, holding up a bloody big toe. But she was not crying; she was actually looking rather frightened.

"Papa, I didn't get any blood on the carpet," she said. I was crushed by the idea that she would be more worried about what I was going to say to her than about her injury.

So I merely said, "Come here, sweetheart, let's put a bandage on it."

I had her sit down and I checked things out. She had torn the toenail, and I knew it had to hurt. So I cleaned her little foot, and then I bandaged it. But as I did, something powerful came over me. I felt as though I was serving this "little one," perhaps the way Jesus would have done.

There are only occasional moments in my life when I feel as filled with joy as I did as I bandaged my Katie's toe. I have no idea whether she understood that. I only hope that she will sometimes remember me that way, as a kind grandfather, ever-so-slightly like Christ. This can be a mean world, where people feel pitted against each other, grasping to get what they can. But it doesn't have to be like that. We're so in need of kindness, and when we're humble—meek—and we let love flow through us, life is simply better, both for us and for those we serve. I want to hold that feeling I had, looking after Katie, and let the feeling lift me.

It *is* that simple. Life is *not* a contest. When we feel the Holy Spirit, that all becomes clear to us. Kindness isn't hard. It's a joy. Life isn't a struggle—not when we remember what we're doing here. We're not climbing over others to get to some mythical top that has never existed. We're *becoming*. And when we give up our pride and listen to the Spirit, the path is easy. We see Who's walking ahead, reaching back for us, and all we have to do is take His hand and follow.

Index

About the Author

DEAN HUGHES HAS PUBLISHED more than ninety books and numerous stories and poems for readers of all ages—children, young adults, and adults. Among his most popular and well-known books are the series of novels *Children of the Promise* and *Hearts of the Children,* which chronicle events in the lives of the fictional Thomas family and cover the years from 1940 to 1974.

Dr. Hughes received his B.A. from Weber State University in Ogden, Utah, and his M.A. and Ph.D. from the University of Washington in Seattle. He has attended post-doctoral seminars at Stanford and Yale Universities and has taught English at Central Missouri State University and Brigham Young University.

He has also served in many callings in The Church of Jesus Christ of Latter-day Saints, including that of a bishop. He and his wife, Kathleen Hurst Hughes, a former counselor in the general Relief Society presidency, have three children and nine grandchildren. They reside in Midway, Utah.